Sew Happy

10 Cheerful Quilts You'll Have Fun Making

Sandy Klop
of American Jane

Martingale®
Create with Confidence

Sew Happy: 10 Cheerful Quilts You'll Have Fun Making
© 2020 by Sandy Klop

Martingale®
19021 120th Ave. NE, Ste. 102
Bothell, WA 98011-9511 USA
ShopMartingale.com

Printed in Hong Kong
25 24 23 22 21 20   8 7 6 5 4 3 2 1

Library of Congress Cataloging-in-Publication Data is available upon request.

ISBN: 978-1-68356-083-8

MISSION STATEMENT

We empower makers who use fabric and yarn to make life more enjoyable.

CREDITS

PUBLISHER AND CHIEF VISIONARY OFFICER
Jennifer Erbe Keltner

CONTENT DIRECTOR
Karen Costello Soltys

DESIGN MANAGER
Adrienne Smitke

MANAGING EDITOR
Tina Cook

PRODUCTION MANAGER
Regina Girard

ACQUISITIONS AND DEVELOPMENT EDITOR
Laurie Baker

COVER AND BOOK DESIGNER
Mia Mar

TECHNICAL EDITOR
Nancy Mahoney

PHOTOGRAPHER
Brent Kane

COPY EDITOR
Melissa Bryan

ILLUSTRATOR
Sandy Loi

SPECIAL THANKS
Photography for this book was taken at the homes of Bree Larson, Everett, Washington, and Stephanie Sullivan, Issaquah, Washington.

Contents

Introduction

I love working with color! Bright, pure colors, mixed and matched with lots of prints, make my heart sing. Perhaps it all relates back to my days as a primary-grade art teacher, but primary colors, polka dots, checks, and fun prints all work together to make fun and cheerful quilts.

When it comes to colors, I think most people notice that my favorite color is red. I use it in so many of my designs. So don't be surprised when you see Yellow Patty Lucy on page 46, as there are no red fabrics in sight! But regardless of what I like, be true to yourself and use *your* favorite colors. Most of the quilts in this book are rather easy to make, so why not mix things up and change the color palette to one that makes you feel joyful?

This book is like a trip down memory lane. I've pulled together a collection of quilts that I've made over the years. So you'll see some older fabrics as well as some newer ones, but overall, the collection feels timeless. You can make your renditions of any of these quilts by digging through your stash or choosing the latest collection of fabrics from your favorite quilt shop. I find the more fabrics you use, the merrier your quilt will be. Happy sewing!

~ Sandy

Checks Mix

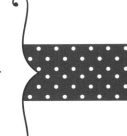

Mix the checks and add three other simple blocks to spice them up. Toss together, bake, and enjoy! This quilt was made using 25-Patch exchange blocks. Adding the setting blocks in red and cream gave me a way to design a larger quilt and put my own spin on things!

Materials

Yardage is based on 42"-wide fabric.

- 4¼ yards of muslin for blocks
- 2⅜ yards *total* of assorted prints for blocks
- 1½ yards of red pindot for blocks*
- 2⅜ yards of red floral for border
- ⅝ yard of black print for binding
- 7¼ yards of fabric for backing
- 86" × 86" piece of batting

*You may want to use more than one red print, as I did.

Cutting

All measurements include ¼" seam allowances.

From the muslin, cut:

56 strips, 1¾" × 42"

3 strips, 6¾" × 42"; crosscut into 50 rectangles, 1¾" × 6¾"

4 strips, 4¼" × 42"; crosscut into 50 rectangles, 3" × 4¼"

From the assorted prints, cut a *total* of:

39 strips, 1¾" × 42"

From the red pindot, cut:

7 strips, 4¼" × 42"; crosscut *3 of the strips* into 64 rectangles, 1¾" × 4¼"

10 strips, 1¾" × 42"

From the *lengthwise* grain of the red floral, cut:

4 strips, 4½" × 81"

From the black print, cut:

8 strips, 2¼" × 42"

Making the Strip Sets

Press all seam allowances in the directions indicated by the arrows.

1 Arrange three different print and two muslin 1¾" × 42" strips as shown. Sew the strips together to make a strip set measuring 6¾" × 42", including seam allowances. Make a total of nine strip sets. Crosscut the strip sets into 180 segments, 1¾" × 6¾", for block A.

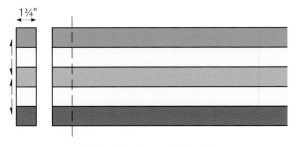

Make 9 strip sets, 6¾" × 42".
Cut 180 segments, 1¾" × 6¾".

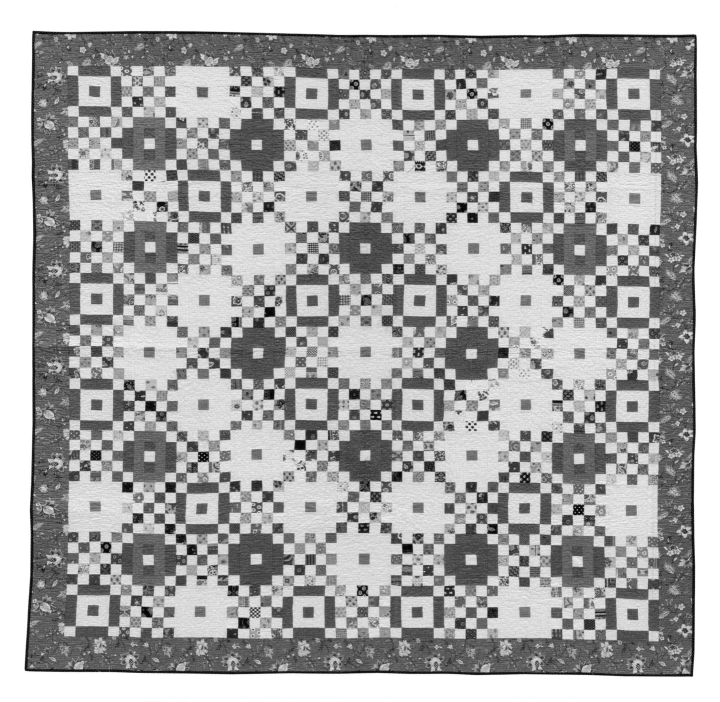

Finished quilt: 77¼" × 77¼"   Finished blocks: 6¼" × 6¼"

2 Arrange three muslin and two different print 1¾" × 42" strips as shown. Sew the strips together to make a strip set measuring 6¾" × 42", including seam allowances. Make a total of six strip sets. Crosscut the strip sets into 120 segments, 1¾" × 6¾", for block A.

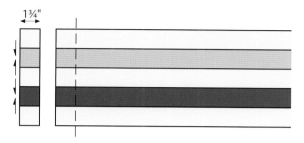

Make 6 strip sets, 6¾" × 42".
Cut 120 segments, 1¾" × 6¾".

3 Sew a muslin 1¾" × 42" strip to each long side of a red pindot 4¼" × 42" strip to make a strip set measuring 6¾" × 42", including seam allowances. Make a total of four strip sets. Crosscut the strip sets into 72 segments, 1¾" × 6¾". You will use 40 segments for block B and 32 segments for block D.

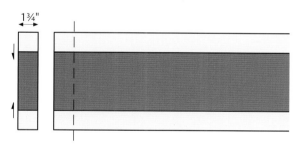

Make 4 strip sets, 6¾" × 42".
Cut 72 segments, 1¾" × 6¾".

4 Join a red pindot and a muslin 1¾" × 42" strip to make a strip set measuring 3" × 42", including seam allowances. Make a total of five strip sets. Crosscut the strip sets into 40 segments, 3" × 4¼", for block B.

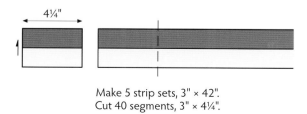

Make 5 strip sets, 3" × 42".
Cut 40 segments, 3" × 4¼".

5 Sew a muslin 1¾" × 42" strip to each long side of a red pindot 1¾" × 42" strip to make a strip set measuring 4¼" × 42", including seam allowances. Make a total of three strip sets. Crosscut the strip sets into 45 segments, 1¾" × 4¼". You will use 20 segments for block B and 25 segments for block C.

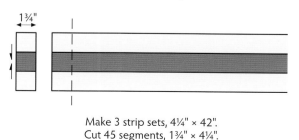

Make 3 strip sets, 4¼" × 42".
Cut 45 segments, 1¾" × 4¼".

6 Sew a red pindot 1¾" × 42" strip to each long side of the remaining muslin 1¾" × 42" strip to make a strip set measuring 4¼" × 42", including seam allowances. Crosscut the strip set into 16 segments, 1¾" × 4¼", for block D.

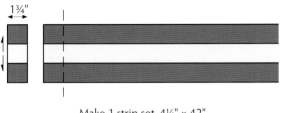

Make 1 strip set, 4¼" × 42".
Cut 16 segments, 1¾" × 4¼".

Making the Blocks

Use the segments from "Making the Strip Sets" to make the following blocks.

1 Lay out three segments from step 1 and two segments from step 2, starting and ending with a step 1 segment. Join the segments to make an A block measuring 6¾" square, including seam allowances. Make 60 blocks.

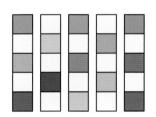

Block A.
Make 60 blocks,
6¾" × 6¾".

2 Lay out two segments from step 3, two segments from step 4, and one segment from step 5 as shown, above right. Join the

segments to make a B block measuring 6¾" square, including seam allowances. Make 20 blocks.

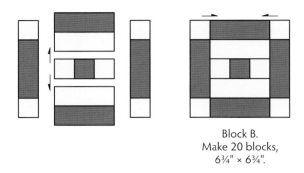

Block B.
Make 20 blocks,
6¾" × 6¾".

3 Lay out two muslin 1¾" × 6¾" rectangles, two muslin 3" × 4¼" rectangles, and one segment from step 5. Join the pieces to make a C block measuring 6¾" square, including seam allowances. Make 25 blocks.

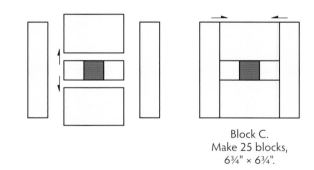

Block C.
Make 25 blocks,
6¾" × 6¾".

4 Sew a segment from step 6 between two red 1¾" × 4¼" rectangles to make a center unit measuring 4¼" square, including seam allowances. Make 16 units.

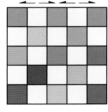
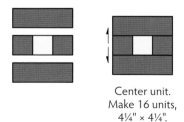

Center unit.
Make 16 units,
4¼" × 4¼".

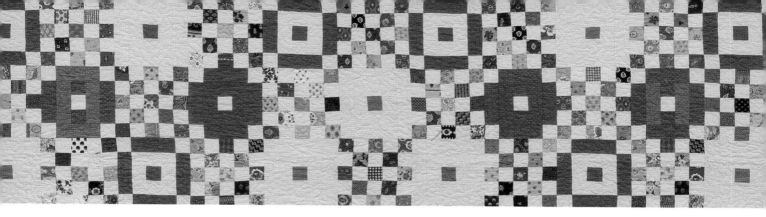

5 Lay out two segments from step 3, two red 1¾" × 4¼" rectangles, and one center unit. Join the pieces to make a D block measuring 6¾" square, including seam allowances. Make 16 blocks.

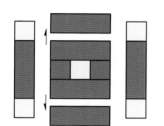
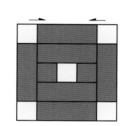

Block D.
Make 16 blocks,
6¾" × 6¾".

Assembling the Quilt Top

1 Lay out the A, B, C, and D blocks in 11 rows of 11 blocks each as shown in the quilt assembly diagram below, rotating the A blocks as desired. Sew the blocks into rows. Join the rows to complete the quilt-top center measuring 69¼" square, including seam allowances.

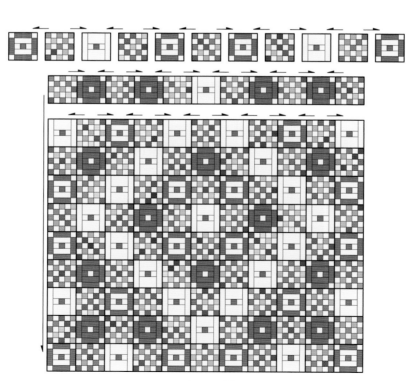

Quilt assembly

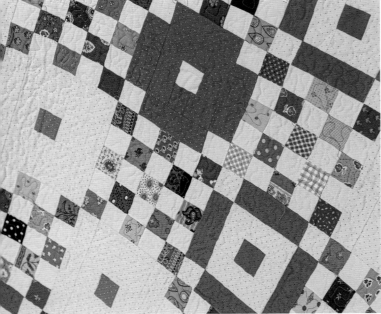

2 Center and then sew a red floral strip to each side of the quilt, stopping ¼" from each corner. Use your preferred method to miter the corners. For more help with the mitered borders, go to ShopMartingale.com/HowtoQuilt. The completed quilt top should measure 77¼" square.

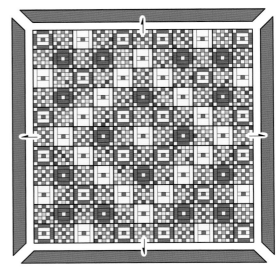

Add borders

Finishing the Quilt

For more details on any of the finishing steps, go to ShopMartingale.com/HowtoQuilt to download free illustrated information.

1 Layer the backing, batting, and quilt top; baste.

2 Hand or machine quilt. The quilt shown is machine quilted using an allover design of loops and swirls.

3 Use the black 2¼"-wide strips to make binding, and then attach the binding to the quilt.

Birds and Boughs

To quote musician Greg Champion, "Keep a green bough in heart and the singing bird will come." These birds and boughs will warm your heart and home, so listen for that singing bird.

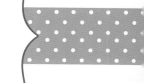

Materials

Yardage is based on 42"-wide fabric. Fat quarters measure 18" × 21"; fat eighths measure 9" × 21".

- 3½ yards of cream solid for background and border
- 1 fat quarter of red print A for Star blocks and small circles
- 8" × 8" square of red plaid for Star block centers
- 4" × 8" rectangle of black print A for Star block centers
- 1 fat quarter of black print B for vines
- ¾ yard of red print B for large heart, flower buds, and binding
- 1 fat eighth of red check for medium heart
- 1 fat eighth of gold plaid for basket
- 1 fat eighth of blue print for large bird bodies
- 5 fat eighths of assorted green prints for leaves
- Assorted print scraps in red, gold, blue, and white for large bird heads and wings, small bird bodies and wings, small hearts, small circles, and large circles
- 3½ yards of fabric for backing
- 61" × 73" piece of batting
- 2½ yards of paper-backed fusible web (optional)
- ¼"-wide bias bar for vines
- Black thread or embroidery floss
- Cardstock
- Spray starch

Cutting

All measurements include ¼" seam allowances.

From the *lengthwise* grain of the cream solid, cut:

1 piece, 42" × 44"; crosscut into:
    1 strip, 11½" × 43½"
    1 strip, 13½" × 43½"
    2 strips, 6½" × 42½"

1 piece, 42" × 67"; crosscut into:
    2 strips, 6½" × 66½"
    1 rectangle, 25½" × 32½"
    4 rectangles, 3" × 9½"
    24 squares, 3½" × 3½"
    12 squares, 4¼" × 4¼". Cut the squares into quarters diagonally to yield 48 triangles.

Continued on page 14

Continued from page 13

From red print A, cut:

3 strips, 4¼" × 21"; crosscut into 12 squares, 4¼" × 4¼". Cut the squares into quarters diagonally to yield 48 triangles.

From the red plaid, cut:

4 squares, 3½" × 3½"

From black print A, cut:

2 squares, 3½" × 3½"

From black print B, cut on the *bias*:

3 strips, 1" × 24"

8 strips, 1" × 11"

4 strips, 1" × 5"

From red print B, cut:

7 strips, 2¼" × 42"

Making the Star Blocks

Press all seam allowances in the directions indicated by the arrows.

1 Lay out two cream triangles and two red A triangles in alternating positions. Sew the triangles together into pairs. Join the pairs to make an hourglass unit measuring 3½" square, including seam allowances. Make 24 units.

Make 24 units, 3½" × 3½".

2 Lay out four cream 3½" squares, four hourglass units, and one red plaid square in three rows, rotating each hourglass unit so that a cream triangle is adjacent to the center square. Sew the pieces into rows. Join the rows to make a block measuring 9½" square, including seam allowances. Make four blocks. Repeat to make two blocks using the black A squares instead of the red plaid squares.

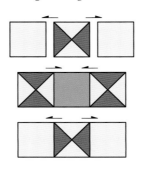 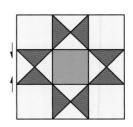

Make 4 blocks, 9½" × 9½".

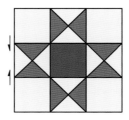

Make 2 blocks, 9½" × 9½".

Qq
is for Quarter Squares

Don't be intimidated by sewing with quarter-square triangles. Just be sure to cut accurately from corner to corner when you're slicing your squares in half diagonally in each direction. For extra insurance, you can cut the squares a bit oversized to start (cut 4½" rather than 4¼") and then trim the finished units to 3½". This gives you some wiggle room!

Finished quilt: 54½" × 66½"   **Finished Star blocks: 9" × 9"**

Appliquéing the Designs

There are several ways to appliqué; use the method of your choice. For the quilt shown, I used a combination of methods. The hearts and large leaves are appliquéd by hand using freezer paper. The small leaves and all the birds are created with fusible appliqué. For more details on appliqué techniques as well as hand embroidery, visit ShopMartingale.com/HowtoQuilt for free downloadable information.

1. Using the patterns on pages 20–23 and referring to the materials list on page 13, prepare the appliqué shapes using your favorite method. If you like to appliqué by hand, add a seam allowance. For both hand and fusible appliqué, you'll need to reverse the patterns as noted for mirror-image shapes. All other shapes are symmetrical and do not need to be reversed.

2. Fold each black B 1"-wide strip in half, wrong sides together, and stitch a scant ¼" from the raw edges. Trim the seam allowance to ⅛". Slide the bias bar inside the fabric tube. Twist the fabric until the seam is centered along one flat side of the bias bar. Press the tube flat, with the seam allowances pressed to one side. Gently work the bias bar through the tube, pressing as you go. When the entire tube has been pressed, remove the bias bar and gently press the tube again.

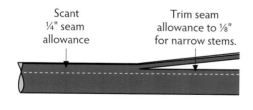

Scant ¼" seam allowance

Trim seam allowance to ⅛" for narrow stems.

Bias bar

3. To make the berries and flower centers, trace four large and 14 small circles onto cardstock. Cut out the circles on the traced lines. Trace the large and small circles onto the wrong side of the chosen prints, leaving at least ⅝" between them. Cut out the circles, adding a generous ¼" seam allowance to each.

4. Sew a long running stitch around the edge of a large circle on the right side of the fabric, about ³⁄₁₆" in from the edge. Don't knot the start or end; instead, leave a long tail at each end. Place the cardstock template in the center of the marked circle. Gently pull the thread tails to gather the fabric over the template until it's evenly gathered and taut around the edge of the circle. Smooth out any puckers on the edge. Tie off the threads to hold the gathering firmly in place. Spray with starch and press well. Repeat for the remaining large and small circles.

5. Gently remove the cardstock template from the circles. Tighten the gathering stitches if required to reshape the circles.

6. Refer to the photo on page 16 and the diagrams on page 18 for appliqué placement guidance. Using the cream 11½" × 43½" strip for the top row, the cream 13½" × 43½" strip for the bottom row, and the cream 25½" × 32½" rectangle for the center, position the appliqué shapes on the strips and rectangles. Tuck the ends of the vines under the other shapes and trim the vines as needed. Appliqué the shapes in place.

7 Press and then trim the strips and rectangles to the sizes indicated, keeping the designs centered.

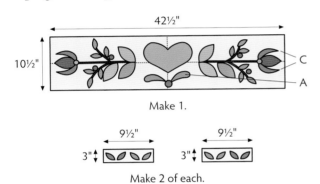

42½"

10½"

C
A

Make 1.

9½" 9½"

3" 3"

Make 2 of each.

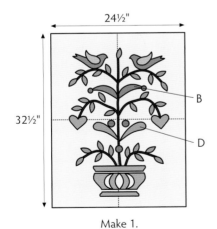

24½"

32½"

B

D

Make 1.

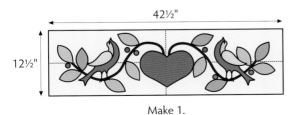

42½"

12½"

Make 1.

8 Stitch the eyes, legs, and feet on the large birds by hand or machine. For hand embroidery, use black floss and a stem stitch.

Assembling the Quilt Top

Refer to the quilt photo as needed throughout.

1 Join three Star blocks, two with red centers and one with a black center, and two 3" × 9½" appliquéd rectangles with reversed leaf colors to make a 9½" × 32½" column, including seam allowances. Make a second column, reversing the leaf colors.

Make 2 columns,
9½" × 32½".

2 Lay out the columns from step 1 and the remaining appliquéd pieces as shown in the quilt assembly diagram below. Sew the columns to the center rectangle. Add the appliquéd top and bottom strips to complete the quilt-top center measuring 42½" × 54½", including seam allowances.

3 Sew the cream 6½" × 42½" strips to the top and bottom of the quilt top. Sew the cream 6½" × 66½" strips to the sides of the quilt top. The completed quilt top should measure 54½" × 66½".

Finishing the Quilt

For more details on any finishing steps, visit ShopMartingale.com/HowtoQuilt for free downloadable information.

1 Layer the backing, batting, and quilt top; baste.

2 Quilt by hand or machine. The quilt shown is machine quilted with a diagonal grid in the center. Swirls and loops are quilted in the star columns and in the top and bottom appliquéd sections. A feather motif is quilted in the border.

3 Use the red B 2¼"-wide strips to make the binding, and then attach the binding to the quilt.

Quilt assembly

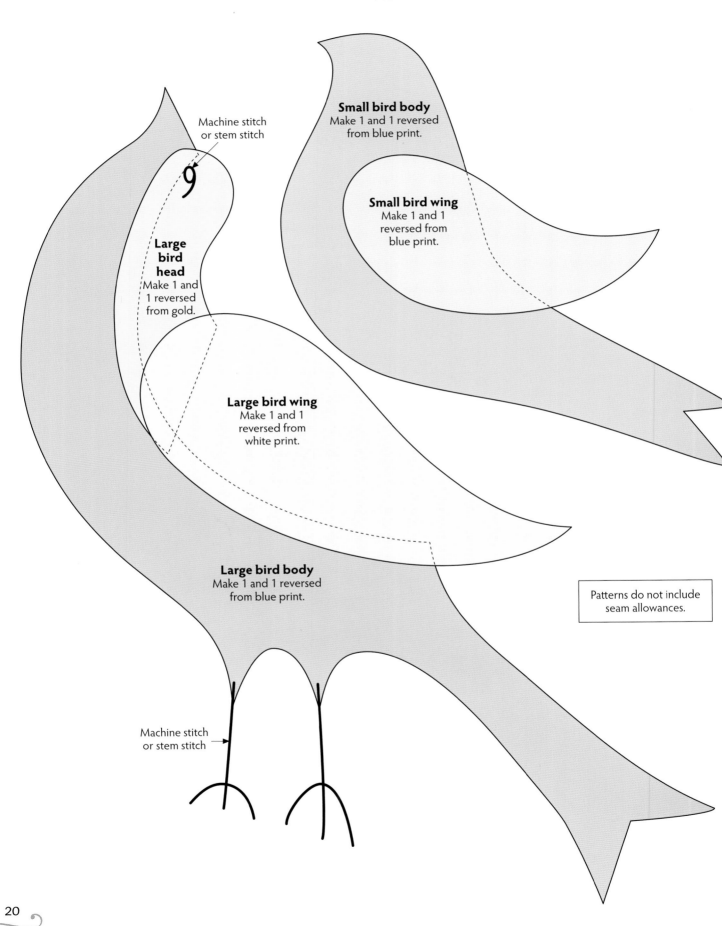

Machine stitch
or stem stitch

9

**Large
bird
head**
Make 1 and
1 reversed
from gold.

Small bird body
Make 1 and 1 reversed
from blue print.

Small bird wing
Make 1 and 1
reversed from
blue print.

Large bird wing
Make 1 and 1
reversed from
white print.

Large bird body
Make 1 and 1 reversed
from blue print.

Patterns do not include
seam allowances.

Machine stitch
or stem stitch

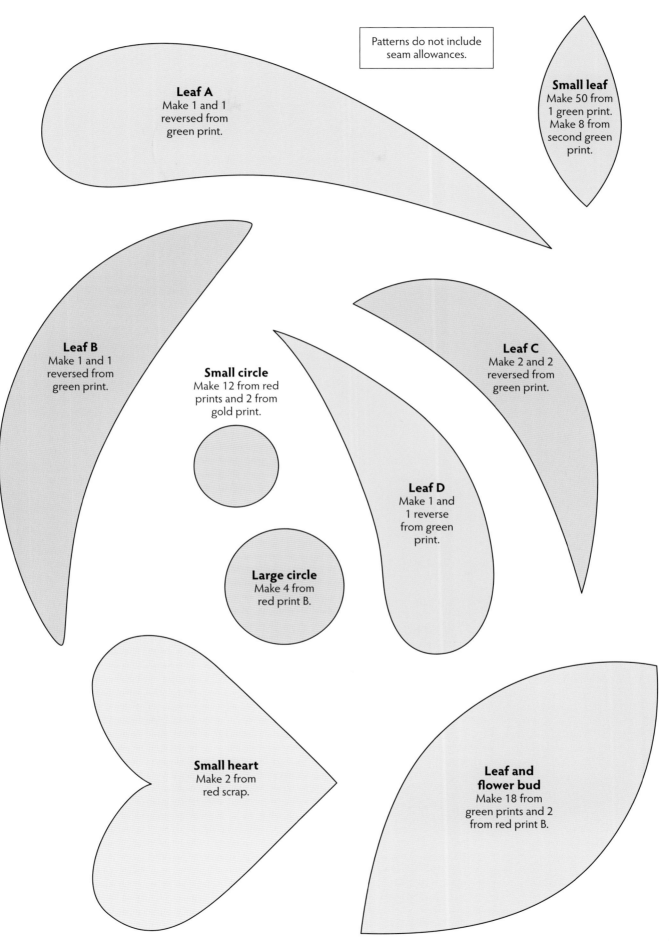

Patterns do not include seam allowances.

Small leaf
Make 50 from 1 green print. Make 8 from second green print.

Leaf A
Make 1 and 1 reversed from green print.

Leaf B
Make 1 and 1 reversed from green print.

Small circle
Make 12 from red prints and 2 from gold print.

Leaf C
Make 2 and 2 reversed from green print.

Leaf D
Make 1 and 1 reverse from green print.

Large circle
Make 4 from red print B.

Small heart
Make 2 from red scrap.

Leaf and flower bud
Make 18 from green prints and 2 from red print B.

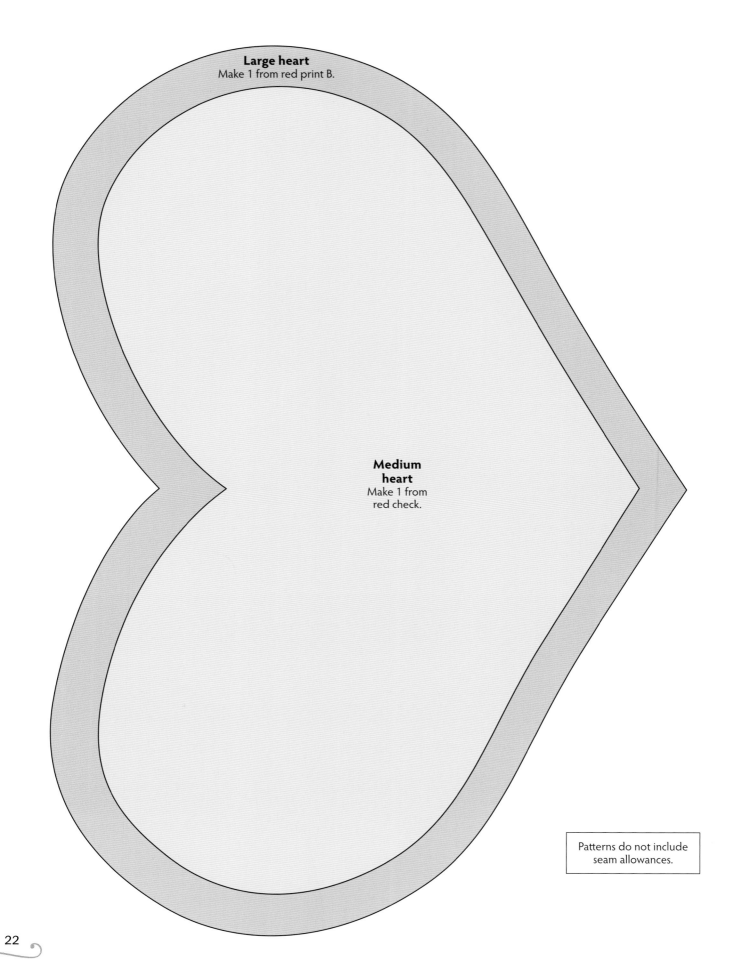

Large heart
Make 1 from red print B.

**Medium
heart**
Make 1 from
red check.

Patterns do not include
seam allowances.

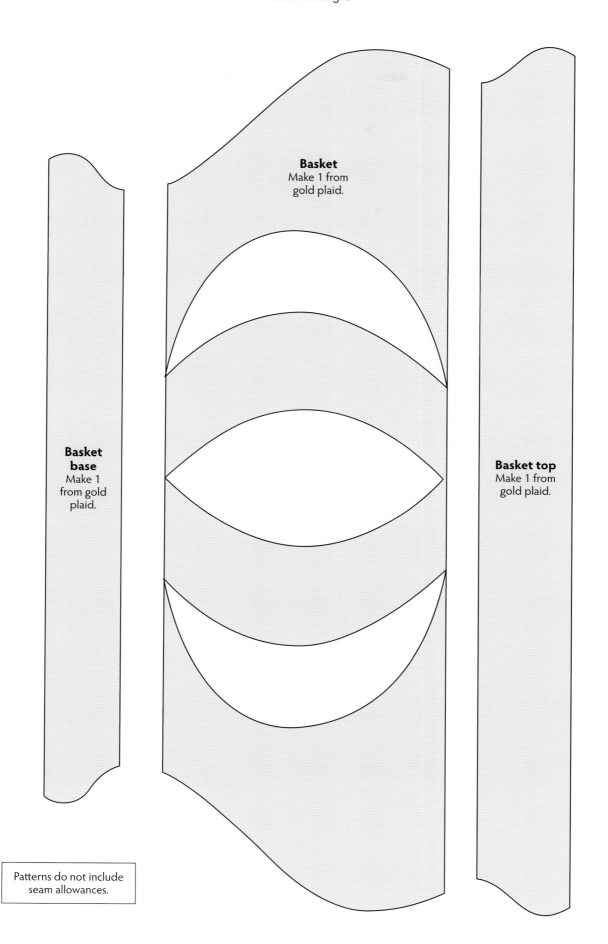

Basket
Make 1 from
gold plaid.

**Basket
base**
Make 1
from gold
plaid.

Basket top
Make 1 from
gold plaid.

Patterns do not include
seam allowances.

Little Sister

As soon as I saw the antique version of this Nine Patch quilt, I knew I had to make one like it! The charming checkerboard center is constructed from simple nine patches, but the colors are offset to create a diagonal effect. The unusual border was a "must have." This is for my newest granddaughter—the little sister of my first one.

Materials

Yardage is based on 42"-wide fabric. Fat quarters measure 18" × 21"; fat eighths measure 9" × 21".

- 3¾ yards of muslin for blocks and borders
- ¼ yard *total* of assorted pink prints for blocks
- ½ yard *total* of assorted red prints for blocks
- ⅞ yard *total* of assorted blue prints for blocks
- ¼ yard *each* of 6 assorted orange prints for blocks and pieced border
- ⅝ yard *total* of assorted aqua prints for blocks
- ¼ yard *total* of assorted green prints for blocks
- ¼ yard *total* of assorted yellow prints for blocks
- ½ yard of orange stripe for binding
- 3⅞ yards of fabric for backing
- 68" × 68" piece of batting

Ff

is for Fabric Choices

To make the quilt look old, I purposely "ran out" of fabrics and mingled different prints of similar colors. Notice the various oranges in the border, where I used a total of four different orange fabrics. You could also do something similar with the Nine Patch blocks.

Cutting

All measurements include ¼" seam allowances.

From the muslin, cut:
80 strips, 1½" × 42"; crosscut *6 of the strips* into:
   8 strips, 1½" × 21"
   4 rectangles, 1½" × 3½"
   12 rectangles, 1½" × 2½"
   16 squares, 1½" × 1½"

From the pink prints (A), cut a *total* of:
5 strips, 1½" × 42"

From the red prints (B), cut a *total* of:
10 strips, 1½" × 42"

From the blue prints (C), cut a *total* of:
15 strips, 1½" × 42"

From the orange prints (D), cut a *total* of:
19 strips, 1½" × 42"; crosscut *2 of the strips* into:
   32 squares, 1½" × 1½"
   4 rectangles, 1½" × 3½"
4 strips, 3½" × 42"

From the aqua prints (E), cut a *total* of:
11 strips, 1½" × 42"

From the green prints (F), cut a *total* of:
3 strips, 1½" × 42"; crosscut into 6 strips, 1½" × 21"
   (1 is extra)

From the yellow prints (G), cut a *total* of:
3 strips, 1½" × 42"; crosscut into 6 strips, 1½" × 21"
   (1 is extra)

From the orange stripe, cut:
7 strips, 2¼" × 42"

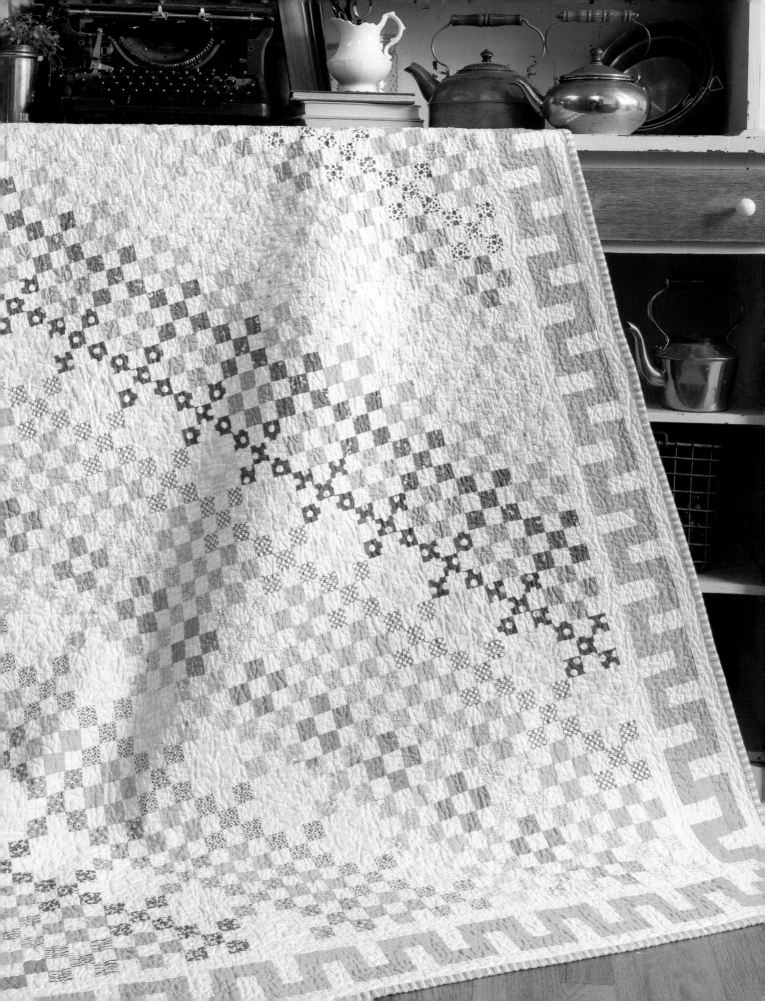

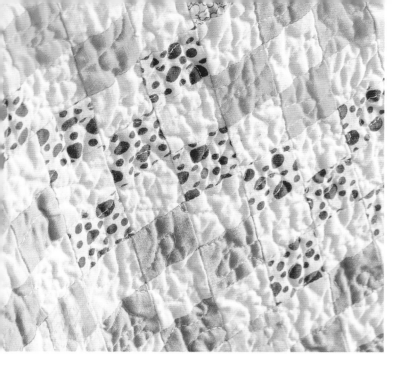

Making the Blocks

Press all seam allowances in the directions indicated by the arrows.

1 Sew a pink strip to each long side of a muslin 1½" × 42" strip to make a strip set measuring 3½" × 42", including seam allowances. Make a total of two strip sets. Crosscut the strip sets into 36 segments, 1½" × 3½".

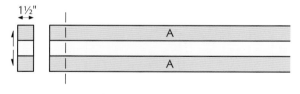

Make 2 strip sets, 3½" × 42".
Cut 36 segments, 1½" × 3½".

2 Sew a muslin 1½" × 42" strip to each long side of the remaining pink strip to make a strip set measuring 3½" × 42", including seam allowances. Crosscut the strip set into 18 segments, 1½" × 3½".

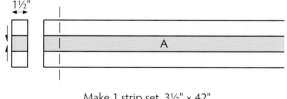

Make 1 strip set, 3½" × 42".
Cut 18 segments, 1½" × 3½".

3 In the same way, make the number of strip sets shown for each color. Crosscut the strip sets into the number of 1½"-wide segments indicated below.

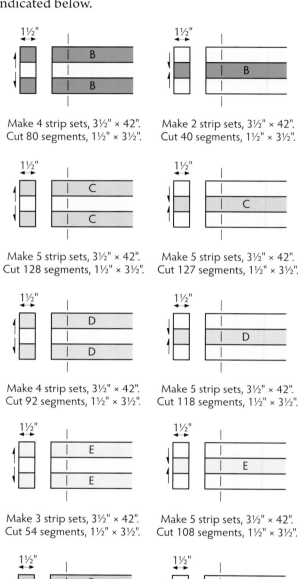

Make 4 strip sets, 3½" × 42".
Cut 80 segments, 1½" × 3½".

Make 2 strip sets, 3½" × 42".
Cut 40 segments, 1½" × 3½".

Make 5 strip sets, 3½" × 42".
Cut 128 segments, 1½" × 3½".

Make 5 strip sets, 3½" × 42".
Cut 127 segments, 1½" × 3½".

Make 4 strip sets, 3½" × 42".
Cut 92 segments, 1½" × 3½".

Make 5 strip sets, 3½" × 42".
Cut 118 segments, 1½" × 3½".

Make 3 strip sets, 3½" × 42".
Cut 54 segments, 1½" × 3½".

Make 5 strip sets, 3½" × 42".
Cut 108 segments, 1½" × 3½".

Make 2 strip sets, 3½" × 21".
Cut 20 segments, 1½" × 3½".

Make 1 strip set, 3½" × 21".
Cut 10 segments, 1½" × 3½".

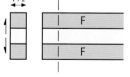

Make 2 strip sets, 3½" × 21".
Cut 24 segments, 1½" × 3½".

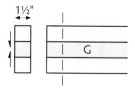

Make 1 strip set, 3½" × 21".
Cut 12 segments, 1½" × 3½".

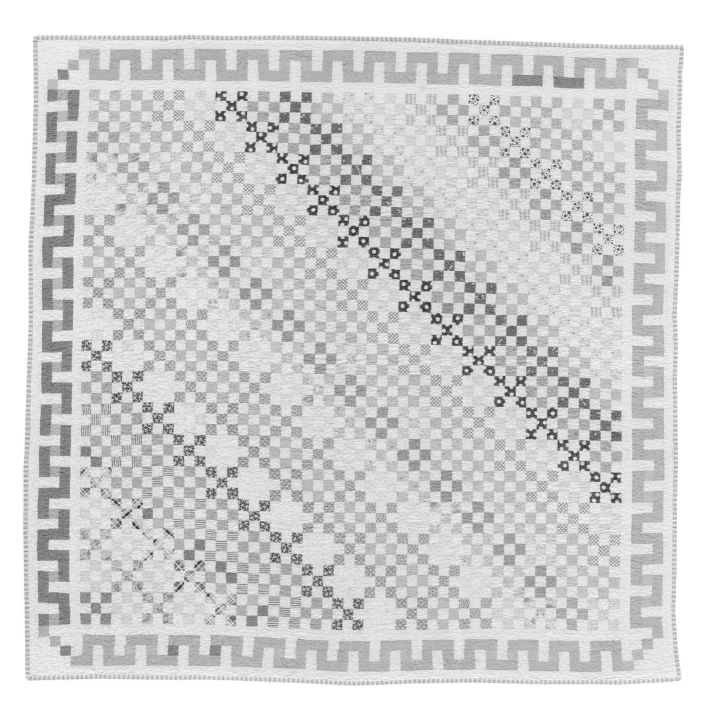

Finished quilt: 61½" × 61½"   **Finished blocks: 3" × 3"**

4 Join two segments with one muslin square and one segment with two muslin squares to make a Nine Patch block measuring 3½" square, including seam allowances. Make the number of blocks for each color as shown and label each colorway by block letter for easier quilt assembly.

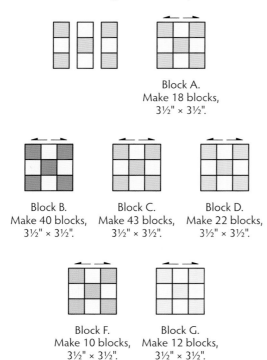

Block A.
Make 18 blocks,
3½" × 3½".

Block B.
Make 40 blocks,
3½" × 3½".

Block C.
Make 43 blocks,
3½" × 3½".

Block D.
Make 22 blocks,
3½" × 3½".

Block F.
Make 10 blocks,
3½" × 3½".

Block G.
Make 12 blocks,
3½" × 3½".

5 Join two segments with two muslin squares and one segment with one muslin square to make a Nine Patch block measuring 3½" square, including seam allowances. Make the number of blocks shown for each color and label each colorway by block letter.

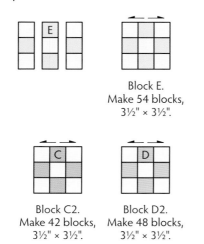

Block E.
Make 54 blocks,
3½" × 3½".

Block C2.
Make 42 blocks,
3½" × 3½".

Block D2.
Make 48 blocks,
3½" × 3½".

Making the Pieced Greek Key Border

1 Join two orange and two muslin 1½" × 42" strips to make a strip set measuring 4½" × 42", including seam allowances. Make a total of two strip sets. Crosscut the strip sets into 48 segments, 1½" × 4½".

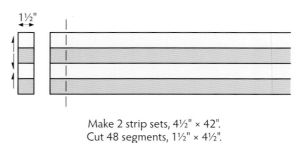

Make 2 strip sets, 4½" × 42".
Cut 48 segments, 1½" × 4½".

2 Sew a muslin 1½" × 42" strip to one long side of an orange 3½" × 42" strip to make a strip set measuring 4½" × 42", including seam allowances. Make a total of four strip sets. Crosscut the strip sets into 96 segments, 1½" × 4½".

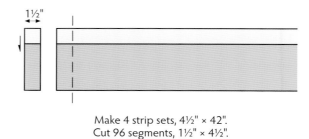

Make 4 strip sets, 4½" × 42".
Cut 96 segments, 1½" × 4½".

3 Join one muslin and one orange square to make a two-patch unit measuring 1½" × 2½", including seam allowances. Make four units.

Make 4 units,
1½" × 2½".

4 Join one muslin and two orange squares to make a three-patch unit measuring 1½" × 3½", including seam allowances. Make four units.

Make 4 units,
1½" × 3½".

5 Join one orange square and one muslin 1½" × 2½" rectangle to make an end unit measuring 1½" × 3½", including seam allowances. Make eight units.

Make 8 units,
1½" × 3½".

6 Join 12 segments from step 2, one orange square, and one two-patch unit from step 3 to make a strip measuring 1½" × 51½", including seam allowances. Make four strips.

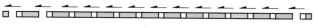

Make 4 strips,
1½" × 51½".

7 Join 12 segments from step 1 and one three-patch unit from step 4 to make a strip measuring 1½" × 51½", including seam allowances. Make four strips.

Make 4 strips,
1½" × 51½".

8 Join 12 segments from step 2 and one orange rectangle to make a strip measuring 1½" × 51½", including seam allowances. Make four strips.

Make 4 strips,
1½" × 51½".

9 Join one strip each from steps 6, 7, and 8 to make a border unit. Sew an end unit from step 5 to each end of the border unit to make a border strip measuring 3½" × 53½", including seam allowances. Make four border strips.

Make 4 borders,
3½" × 53½".

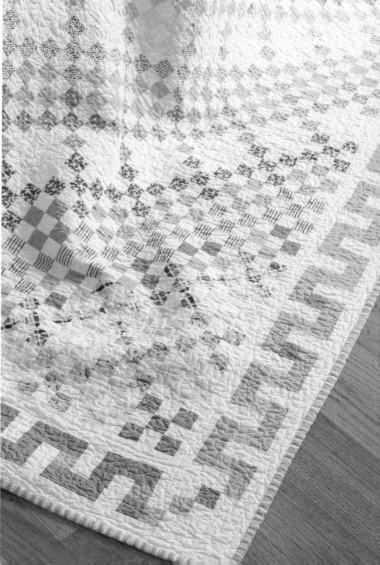

⑩ Join two muslin and two orange squares to make a four-patch unit measuring 2½" square, including seam allowances. Sew a muslin 1½" × 2½" rectangle to the top of the unit. Then sew a muslin 1½" × 3½" rectangle to the left side to make a corner block measuring 3½" square, including seam allowances. Make four blocks.

Corner block
Make 4 blocks,
3½" × 3½".

Assembling the Quilt Top

Refer to the photo on page 27 as needed throughout.

① Referring to the quilt assembly diagram below, lay out the blocks in 17 rows of 17 blocks each, following the block labels and colors as shown.

② When you are pleased with the arrangement, sew the blocks into horizontal rows. Join the rows to make a quilt-top center measuring 51½" square, including seam allowances.

③ Sew the remaining muslin strips end to end. From the pieced strip, cut two 61½"-long strips, two 59½"-long strips, two 53½"-long strips, and two 51½" long strips.

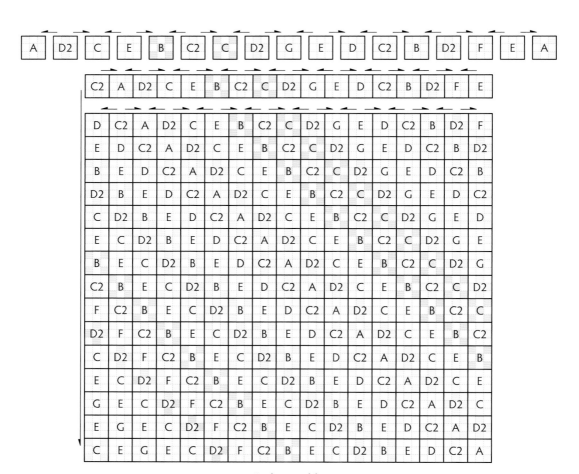

Quilt assembly

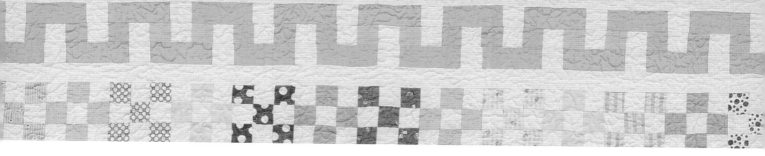

4 Sew the muslin 51½"-long strips to opposite sides of the quilt-top center. Sew the 53½"-long strips to the top and bottom. The quilt top should measure 53½" square, including seam allowances.

5 Sew pieced border strips to opposite sides of the quilt top. Note that the strips from step 8 on page 29 are joined to the quilt center on all sides. This will make the Greek Key effect work at the border corners. Sew a corner block to each end of the remaining pieced borders. Sew these border strips to the top and bottom of the quilt top. The quilt top should measure 59½" square, including seam allowances.

6 Sew the muslin 59½"-long strips to opposite sides of the quilt top. Sew the 61½"-long strips to the top and bottom. The completed quilt top should measure 61½" square.

Finishing the Quilt

For more details on any finishing steps, visit ShopMartingale.com/HowtoQuilt for free downloadable information.

1 Layer the backing, batting, and quilt top; baste.

2 Quilt by hand or machine. The quilt shown is machine quilted with an allover meandering design.

3 Use the orange stripe 2¼"-wide strips to make the binding, and then attach the binding to the quilt.

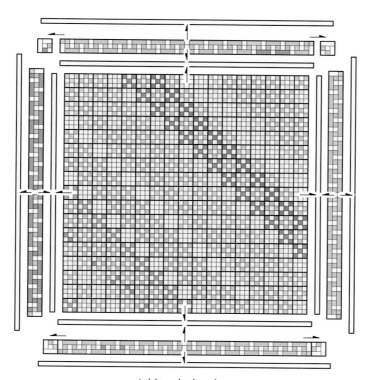

Adding the borders

Gramma's Kitchen

In my grandmother's red-and-white kitchen was a small door, next to the kitchen table, where the milkman would put two glass bottles of cold white milk. The memory of that cold milk on a hot summer day in Gramma's kitchen makes my head spin like these pinwheels. Give your table a crisp vintage look as refreshing as a glass of milk.

Materials

Yardage is based on 42"-wide fabric.

- 1⅞ yards of white print for blocks
- ⅝ yard of yellow print for blocks
- ⅝ yard of red print for blocks
- ⅜ yard of navy floral for blocks
- ⅜ yard of white floral for blocks
- ½ yard of green floral for blocks
- 1⅛ yard of pink print for blocks
- ¾ yard of cream dot for border
- ½ yard of green dot for binding
- 4 yards of fabric for backing
- 72" × 72" piece of batting

Cutting

All measurements include ¼" seam allowances.

From the white print, cut:

18 strips, 3⅜" × 42"; crosscut into 192 squares, 3⅜" × 3⅜". Cut the squares in half diagonally to yield 384 triangles.

From the yellow print, cut:

6 strips, 3⅜" × 42"; crosscut into 64 squares, 3⅜" × 3⅜". Cut the squares in half diagonally to yield 128 triangles.

From the red print, cut:

6 strips, 3⅜" × 42"; crosscut into 64 squares, 3⅜" × 3⅜". Cut the squares in half diagonally to yield 128 triangles.

From the navy floral, cut:

3 strips, 3⅜" × 42"; crosscut into 32 squares, 3⅜" × 3⅜". Cut the squares in half diagonally to yield 64 triangles.

From the white floral, cut:

3 strips, 3⅜" × 42"; crosscut into 32 squares, 3⅜" × 3⅜". Cut the squares in half diagonally to yield 64 triangles.

From the green floral, cut:

5 strips, 3" × 42"; crosscut into 64 squares, 3" × 3"

From the pink print, cut:

6 strips, 5⅞" × 42"; crosscut into 32 squares, 5⅞" × 5⅞". Cut the squares in half diagonally to yield 64 triangles.

From the cream dot, cut:

7 strips, 3¼" × 42"

From the green dot, cut:

7 strips, 2¼" × 42"

Finished quilt: 66" × 66"   Finished blocks: 7½" × 7½"

Making the Blocks

Press all seam allowances in the directions indicated by the arrows.

 Sew a white print triangle and a yellow triangle together along their long edges to make a half-square-triangle unit measuring 3" square, including seam allowances. Make 128 units. In the same way, use the white print and red triangles to make 128 half-square-triangle units.

Make 128 of each unit,
3" × 3".

 Repeat step 1 using the white floral and navy triangles to make 64 half-square-triangle units.

Make 64 units,
3" × 3".

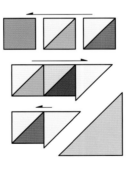 Lay out one green square, two white/yellow units, two white/red units, one white/navy unit, and two white print triangles in three rows. Sew the pieces into rows. Join the rows. Sew a pink triangle to the lower-right corner to make a block measuring 8" square, including seam allowances. Make 64 blocks.

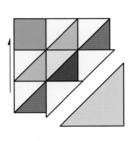

Make 64 blocks,
8" × 8".

2 Join the cream strips end to end. From the pieced strip, cut two 66"-long strips and two 60½"-long strips. Sew the shorter strips to opposite sides of the quilt top. Sew the longer strips to the top and bottom. The completed quilt top should measure 66" square.

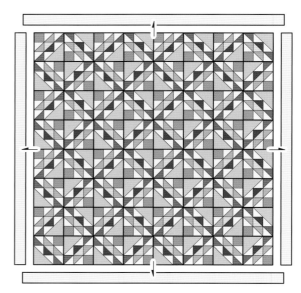

Adding the borders

Assembling the Quilt Top

1 Lay out the blocks in eight rows of eight blocks each, rotating every other block as shown in the quilt assembly diagram. Sew the blocks into rows. Join the rows to complete the quilt-top center measuring 60½" square, including seam allowances.

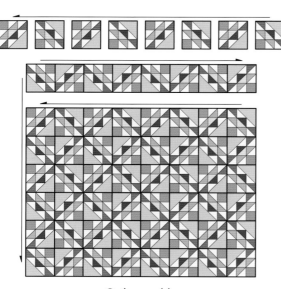

Quilt assembly

Finishing the Quilt

For more details on any finishing steps, visit ShopMartingale.com/HowtoQuilt for free downloadable information.

1 Layer the backing, batting, and quilt top; baste.

2 Quilt by hand or machine. The quilt shown is machine quilted with an allover meandering design.

3 Use the green dot 2¼"-wide strips to make the binding, and then attach the binding to the quilt.

Mistress Mary

Mistress Mary, quite contrary. How does your garden grow?
With silver bells and cockle shells, and pretty maids all in a row.
Who says Snowball blocks have to be snowy? Turn them into
pretty flowers all in a row for a perpetual garden!

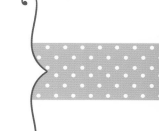

Materials

Yardage is based on 42"-wide fabric. Fat quarters measure 18" × 21".

- 23 fat quarters of assorted 1930s reproduction prints for blocks
- ¼ yard of cream print for blocks
- ¼ yard of burgundy pindot for blocks
- ⅜ yard of orange pindot for blocks
- ½ yard of dark blue pindot for blocks
- ⅝ yard of light yellow pindot for blocks
- ¾ yard of moss green pindot for blocks and stems
- ¾ yard of medium yellow pindot for blocks
- ¾ yard of light blue pindot for blocks
- ⅞ yard of red pindot for blocks
- 1 yard of fern green pindot for blocks
- 1¼ yards of pine green pindot for leaves and binding
- ⅜ yard of muslin for leaves
- ¼ yard of gold pindot for appliquéd circles
- ⅝ yard of green stripe for setting squares
- 7½ yards of fabric for backing
- 89" × 89" piece of batting
- Cardstock
- Spray starch

Cutting

All measurements include ¼" seam allowances.

From the assorted 1930s reproduction prints, cut a *total* of:

221 squares, 4" × 4"

880 squares, 1½" × 1½"

From the cream print, cut:

1 strip, 4" × 42"; crosscut into:

  4 squares, 4" × 4"

  20 squares, 1½" × 1½"

From the burgundy pindot, cut:

1 strip, 4" × 42"; crosscut into 8 squares, 4" × 4"

2 strips, 1½" × 42"; crosscut into 32 squares, 1½" × 1½"

From the orange pindot, cut:

2 strips, 4" × 42"; crosscut into 12 squares, 4" × 4"

2 strips, 1½" × 42"; crosscut into 48 squares, 1½" × 1½"

From the dark blue pindot, cut:

2 strips, 4" × 42"; crosscut into 16 squares, 4" × 4"

3 strips, 1½" × 42"; crosscut into 64 squares, 1½" × 1½"

From the light yellow pindot, cut:

3 strips, 4" × 42"; crosscut into 20 squares, 4" × 4"

4 strips, 1½" × 42"; crosscut into 80 squares, 1½" × 1½"

From the moss green pindot, cut:

4 strips, 4" × 42"; crosscut into:

  24 squares, 4" × 4"

  44 rectangles, 1" × 4"

4 strips, 1½" × 42"; crosscut into 96 squares, 1½" × 1½"

From the medium yellow pindot, cut:

4 strips, 4" × 42"; crosscut into 28 squares, 4" × 4"

5 strips, 1½" × 42"; crosscut into 112 squares, 1½" × 1½"

From the light blue pindot, cut:

4 strips, 4" × 42"; crosscut into 32 squares, 4" × 4"

5 strips, 1½" × 42"; crosscut into 128 squares, 1½" × 1½"

From the red pindot, cut:

4 strips, 4" × 42"; crosscut into 36 squares, 4" × 4"

6 strips, 1½" × 42"; crosscut into 144 squares, 1½" × 1½"

From the fern green pindot, cut:

5 strips, 4" × 42"; crosscut into 40 squares, 4" × 4"

7 strips, 1½" × 42"; crosscut into 160 squares, 1½" × 1½"

From the pine green pindot, cut:

5 strips, 4" × 42"; crosscut into 88 rectangles, 2" × 4"

9 strips, 2¼" × 42"

From the muslin, cut:

7 strips, 1½" × 42"; crosscut into 176 squares, 1½" × 1½"

From the green stripe, cut:

5 strips, 4" × 42"; crosscut into 44 squares, 4" × 4"

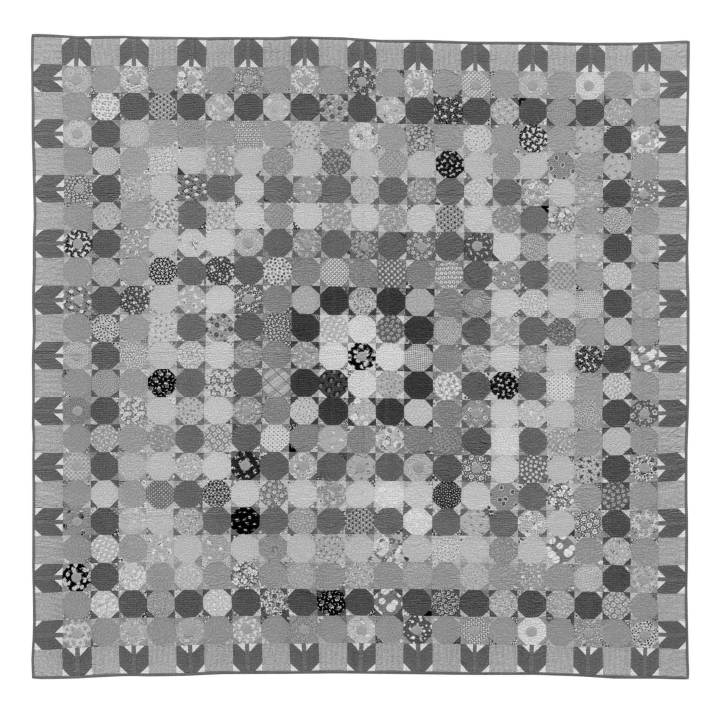

Finished quilt: 81" × 81"   Finished blocks: 3½" × 3½"

Making the A and B Blocks

Press all seam allowances in the directions indicated by the arrows. Note that the dark, bright colors represent the pindot fabrics. The pastel colors represent the reproduction prints throughout.

1 To make the A blocks, draw a diagonal line from corner to corner on the wrong side of the reproduction print 1½" squares. Place a marked square on each corner of a cream 4" square. Sew on the marked lines. Trim the excess corner fabric, ¼" from the stitched line. Make four blocks measuring 4" square, including seam allowances. In the same way, make the number of blocks shown using each color of pindot squares for the block centers.

2 To make the B blocks, draw a diagonal line from corner to corner on the wrong side of the cream and assorted pindot 1½" squares. Using four matching squares, place a marked square on each corner of a reproduction print 4" square. Sew on the marked lines. Trim the excess corner fabric, ¼" from the stitched line. Make five blocks measuring 4" square, including seam allowances. In the same way, make the number of blocks shown using each color of pindot squares for the corners.

Block B.
Make 5 blocks,
4" × 4".

Block A.
Make 4 blocks,
4" × 4".

Make 8
burgundy blocks,
4" × 4".

Make 12
orange blocks,
4" × 4".

Make 16
dark blue blocks,
4" × 4".

Make 8
burgundy blocks,
4" × 4".

Make 12
orange blocks,
4" × 4".

Make 16
dark blue blocks,
4" × 4".

Make 20
light yellow blocks,
4" × 4".

Make 24
moss green blocks,
4" × 4".

Make 28 medium
yellow blocks,
4" × 4".

Make 20
light yellow blocks,
4" × 4".

Make 24
moss green blocks,
4" × 4".

Make 28 medium
yellow blocks,
4" × 4".

Make 32
light blue blocks,
4" × 4".

Make 36
red blocks,
4" × 4".

Make 40
fern green blocks,
4" × 4".

Make 32
light blue blocks,
4" × 4".

Make 36
red blocks,
4" × 4".

Make 40
fern green blocks,
4" × 4".

Making the Leaf Blocks

1. Draw a diagonal line from corner to corner on the wrong side of the muslin 1½" squares. Place marked squares on diagonally opposite corners of a pine green rectangle, making sure to orient the lines as shown. Sew on the marked lines. Trim the excess corner fabric, ¼" from the stitched line. Make 44 leaf units measuring 2" × 4", including seam allowances. Reversing the orientation of the marked squares, make 44 reversed leaf units.

Make 44 of each unit,
2" × 4".

2. Join one leaf unit, one reversed leaf unit, and one moss green rectangle to make a leaf/stem block measuring 4" square, including seam allowances. Make 44 blocks.

Make 44 blocks,
4" × 4".

Appliquéing the Circles

1. Use the pattern on page 45 to trace 57 circles onto cardstock. Cut out the circles on the traced lines. Trace the circles onto the wrong side of the gold pindot, leaving at least ⅝" between them. Cut out the circles, adding a generous ¼" seam allowance to each.

2. Sew a long running stitch around the edges of a circle on the right side of the fabric, about ³⁄₁₆" in from the edge. Don't knot the start or end; instead, leave a long tail at each end. Place the cardstock template in the center of the marked circle. Gently pull the thread tails to gather the fabric over the template until it's evenly gathered and taut around the edge of the circle. Smooth out any puckers on the edge. Tie off the threads to hold the gathering firmly in place. Spray with starch and press well. Repeat for the remaining circles.

3. Gently remove the cardstock template from the circles. Tighten the gathering stitches if required to reshape the circles.

4. Referring to the photo on page 40, position a circle in the center of a B block. Appliqué the circle in place. Make 16 blocks with blue corners, 40 blocks with pine green corners, and one block with cream corners.

Make 16 blocks,   Make 40 blocks,   Make 1 block,
4" × 4".   4" × 4".   4" × 4".

Assembling the Quilt Top

1. Lay out the cream A and B blocks in three rows of three blocks each. Sew the blocks together into rows. Join the rows to make the quilt-top center measuring 11" square, including seam allowances.

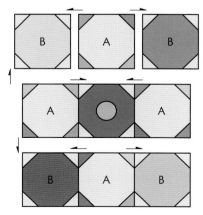

Quilt center

2 Referring to the quilt assembly diagram on page 45 and the quilt photo, join two burgundy A blocks and one burgundy B block to make a side border. Make two and sew them to the quilt center. Join three burgundy B blocks and two burgundy A blocks to make the top border. Repeat to make the bottom border. Sew these borders to the quilt center. The quilt top should measure 18" square, including seam allowance.

Round 1.
Make 2 side borders, 4" × 11".

Round 1.
Make 2 top/bottom borders, 4" × 18".

3 Join three orange A blocks and two orange B blocks to make a side border. Make two and sew them to the quilt top. Join four orange B blocks and three orange A blocks to make the top border. Repeat to make the bottom border. Sew these borders to the quilt center. The quilt top should measure 25" square, including seam allowances.

4 Join four dark blue A blocks and three dark blue B blocks to make a side border. Make two and sew them to the quilt top. Join five dark blue B blocks and four dark-blue A blocks to make the top border. Repeat to make the bottom border. Sew these borders to the quilt center. The quilt top should measure 32" square, including seam allowances.

Round 3.
Make 2 side borders, 4" × 25".

Round 3.
Make 2 top/bottom borders, 4" × 32".

5 Join five light yellow A blocks and four light yellow B blocks to make a side border. Make two and sew them to the quilt top. Join six light yellow B blocks and five light yellow A blocks to make the top border. Repeat to make the bottom border. Sew these borders to the quilt center. The quilt top should measure 39" square, including seam allowances.

Round 4.
Make 2 side borders, 4" × 32".

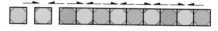

Round 4.
Make 2 top/bottom borders, 4" × 39".

6 Join six moss green A blocks and five moss green B blocks to make a side border. Make two and sew them to the quilt top. Join seven moss green B blocks and six moss green A blocks to make the top border. Repeat to make the bottom border. Sew these borders to the quilt center. The quilt top should measure 46" square, including seam allowances.

Round 5.
Make 2 side borders, 4" × 39".

Round 5.
Make 2 top/bottom borders, 4" × 46".

borders to the quilt center. The quilt top should measure 60" square, including seam allowances.

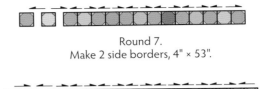

Round 7.
Make 2 side borders, 4" × 53".

Round 7.
Make 2 top/bottom borders, 4" × 60".

9 Join nine red A blocks and eight red B blocks to make a side border. Make two and sew them to the quilt top. Join 10 red B blocks and nine red A blocks to make the top border. Repeat to make the bottom border. Sew these borders to the quilt center. The quilt top should measure 67" square, including seam allowances.

Round 8.
Make 2 side borders, 4" × 60".

Round 8.
Make 2 top/bottom borders, 4" × 67".

10 Join 10 fern green A blocks and nine fern green B blocks to make a side border. Make two and sew them to the quilt top. Join 11 fern green B blocks and 10 fern green A blocks to make the top border. Repeat to make the bottom border. Sew these borders to the quilt center. The quilt top should measure 74" square, including seam allowances.

Round 9.
Make 2 side borders, 4" × 67".

Round 9.
Make 2 top/bottom borders, 4" × 74".

7 Join seven medium yellow A blocks and six medium yellow B blocks to make a side border. Make two and sew them to the quilt top. Join eight medium yellow B blocks and seven medium yellow A blocks to make the top border. Repeat to make the bottom border. Sew these borders to the quilt center. The quilt top should measure 53" square, including seam allowances.

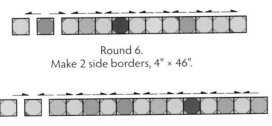

Round 6.
Make 2 side borders, 4" × 46".

Round 6.
Make 2 top/bottom borders, 4" × 53".

8 Join eight light blue A blocks and seven light blue B blocks to make a side border. Make two and sew them to the quilt top. Join nine light blue B blocks and eight light blue A blocks to make the top border. Repeat to make the bottom border. Sew these

11 For the outer border (round 10), join 11 leaf/stem blocks and 10 green stripe squares to make a side border. Make two and sew them to the quilt-top center. Join 12 green stripe squares and 11 leaf/stem blocks to make the top border. Repeat to make the bottom border. Sew these borders to the quilt. The completed quilt top should measure 81" square.

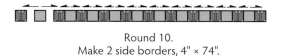

Round 10.
Make 2 side borders, 4" × 74".

Round 10.
Make 2 top/bottom borders, 4" × 81".

Finishing the Quilt

For more details on any finishing steps, visit ShopMartingale.com/HowtoQuilt for free downloadable information.

1 Layer the backing, batting, and quilt top; baste.

2 Quilt by hand or machine. The quilt shown is machine quilted with an allover meandering design.

3 Use the pine green 2¼"-wide strips to make the binding, and then attach the binding to the quilt.

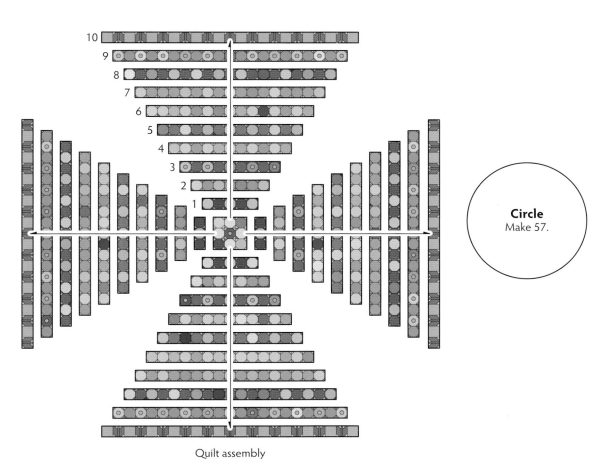

Quilt assembly

Circle
Make 57.

Yellow Patty Lucy

A poem I wrote was the inspiration for this medallion quilt:
A pretty miss all dressed in yellow caught the eye of a handsome
fellow. "What is the color that you are wearing?" she asked
while into his eyes she was staring. "Is it putty or gray?" "Nope,"
he replied. "It's taupe." And filled her heart with hope.

Materials

Yardage is based on 42"-wide fabric.

- ¼ yard *each* of 8 assorted yellow prints for Nine Patch blocks
- 2¼ yards of yellow star print for Star blocks and outer border
- 6 yards of muslin for blocks and borders
- ¼ yard *each* of 9 assorted gray and taupe prints for blocks and border 8
- ⅛ yard of gray stripe for alternate blocks
- ⅞ yard of taupe stripe for border 2 and binding
- ½ yard of gray print for outer border
- 8 yards of fabric for backing
- 96" × 96" piece of batting

Cutting

All measurements include ¼" seam allowances.

From *each* of the assorted yellow prints, cut:

5 strips, 1½" × 42" (40 total; 1 is extra)

From the yellow star print, cut:

8 strips, 2" × 42"; crosscut into 148 squares, 2" × 2"

5 strips, 4¼" × 42"; crosscut into 37 squares, 4¼" × 4¼". Cut the squares into quarters diagonally to yield 148 triangles.

22 strips, 1½" × 42"; crosscut *1* of the strips into 12 squares, 1½" × 1½"

From the muslin, cut:

48 strips, 1½" × 42"; crosscut *1* of the strips into 8 squares, 1½" × 1½"

8 strips, 5½" × 42"; crosscut into 50 squares, 5½" × 5½". Cut the squares into quarters diagonally to yield 200 side triangles.

9 strips, 2⅜" × 42"; crosscut *6* of the strips into:
2 strips, 2⅜" × 26½"
2 strips, 2⅜" × 30¼"
2 strips, 2⅜" × 38¾"

6 strips, 3¼" × 42"

10 strips, 3½" × 42"; crosscut into:
24 rectangles, 3½" × 9½"
4 rectangles, 3½" × 6½"
32 squares, 3½" × 3½"

1 strip, 3" × 42"; crosscut into 12 squares, 3" × 3". Cut the squares in half diagonally to yield 24 corner triangles.

From the assorted gray and taupe prints, cut a *total* of:

37 sets of 4 matching squares, 2⅜" × 2⅜" (148 total); cut the squares in half diagonally to yield 296 small triangles

44 squares, 3½" × 3½"

4 sets of 2 matching squares, 4½" × 4½" (8 total); cut the squares in half diagonally to yield 16 large triangles

Continued on page 49

Finished quilt: 87¼" × 87¼"   Finished blocks: 6" × 6" and 3" × 3"

Continued from page 46

From the gray stripe, cut:

3 strips, ¾" × 42"; crosscut into:

    8 rectangles, ¾" × 6"

    8 rectangles, ¾" × 6½"

From the taupe stripe, cut:

4 strips, 1½" × 42"; crosscut into:

    2 strips, 1½" × 24½"

    2 strips, 1½" × 26½"

9 strips, 2¼" × 42"

From the gray print, cut:

8 strips, 1½" × 42"; crosscut *1* of the strips into

    4 squares, 1½" × 1½"

Making the Nine Patch Blocks

Press all seam allowances in the directions indicated by the arrows.

1 Sew matching yellow strips to each long side of a muslin 1½"-wide strip to make a strip set measuring 3½" × 42", including seam allowances. Make a total of 15 strip sets. Crosscut the strip sets into 388 segments, 1½" × 3½". Keep like segments together.

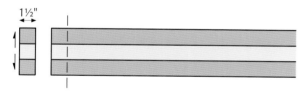

Make 15 strip sets, 3½" × 42".
Cut into 388 segments, 1½" × 3½".

2 Sew a muslin 1½"-wide strip to each long side of a yellow strip to make a strip set measuring 3½" × 42", including seam allowances. Make nine strip sets. Crosscut the strip sets into 215 segments, 1½" × 3½". Keep like segments together.

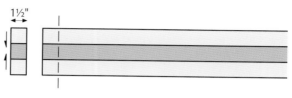

Make 9 strip sets, 3½" × 42".
Cut into 215 segments, 1½" × 3½".

3 Using the same yellow print per block, join two segments from step 1 and one segment from step 2 to make a Nine Patch block measuring 3½" square, including seam allowances. Make 187 blocks and label them block A.

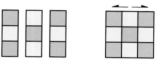

Block A.
Make 187 blocks,
3½" × 3½".

4 Using the same yellow print per block, join two segments from step 2 and one segment from step 1 to make a Nine Patch block measuring 3½" square, including seam allowances. Make 14 blocks and label them block B.

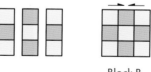

Block B.
Make 14 blocks,
3½" × 3½".

Making the Alternate Blocks

1 Sew matching gray or taupe large triangles to opposite sides of an A block. Sew matching gray or taupe large triangles to the remaining sides of the block to make a center unit. Trim the unit to measure 6" square, including seam allowances. Make four units.

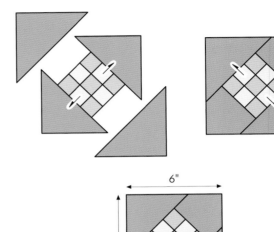

Make 4 units.

Making the Star Blocks

1 Sew matching gray or taupe small triangles to the short sides of a yellow star triangle to make a flying-geese unit measuring 2" × 3½", including seam allowances. Make 37 sets of four matching units (148 total).

Make 37 sets of
4 matching units,
2" × 3½".

2 Lay out four yellow star 2" squares, four matching flying-geese units, and one A block in three rows. Sew the pieces into rows. Join the rows to make a Star block measuring 6½" square, including seam allowances. Make 37 blocks.

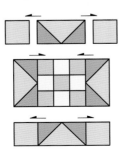 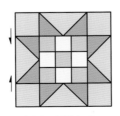

Make 37 blocks,
6½" × 6½".

2 Sew gray striped ¾" × 6" rectangles to opposite sides of a center unit. Sew gray striped ¾" × 6½" rectangles to the top and bottom of the unit to make an alternate block measuring 6½" square, including seam allowances. Make four blocks.

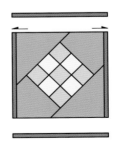 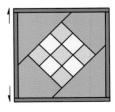

Make 4 blocks,
6½" × 6½".

Assembling the Quilt Center

Lay out five Star blocks and the alternate blocks in three rows of three blocks each, alternating the blocks as shown. Sew the blocks into rows. Join the rows to make the quilt-top center measuring 18½" square, including seam allowances.

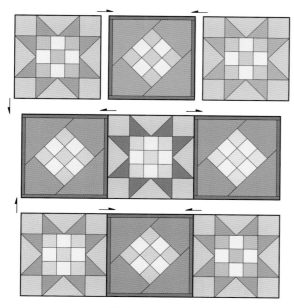

Quilt-top center

Assembling the Quilt Top

Refer to the quilt assembly diagram on page 55 to join the various borders in rounds to the quilt center.

1 For border 1, join three B blocks and three A blocks, starting with a B block and alternating the blocks, to make a side border measuring 3½" × 18½", including seam allowances. Make two. In the same way, join four B blocks and four A blocks to make top/bottom borders measuring 3½" × 24½", including seam allowances. Sew border 1 to the sides first and then to the top

and bottom of the quilt top. The quilt top should measure 24½" square, including seam allowances.

Make 2 side borders,
3½" × 18½".

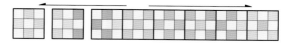

Make 2 top/bottom borders,
3½" × 24½".

2 Sew the taupe striped 1½" × 24½" strips to opposite sides of the quilt top. Sew the taupe striped 1½" × 26½" strips to the top and bottom. The quilt top should measure 26½" square, including seam allowances.

3 Sew the muslin 2⅜" × 26½" strips to opposite sides of the quilt top. Sew the muslin 2⅜" × 30¼" strips to the top and bottom. The quilt top should measure 30¼" square, including seam allowances.

④ For border 4, join seven A blocks, 12 muslin side triangles, and four corner triangles in diagonal rows. Join the rows and remaining corner triangles to make a side border measuring 4¾" × 30¼", including seam allowances. Make two. In the same way, join nine A blocks, 16 muslin side triangles, and four corner triangles to make top/bottom borders measuring 4¾" × 38¾", including seam allowances. Sew border 4 to the sides first and then to the top and bottom of the quilt top. The quilt top should measure 38¾" square, including seam allowances.

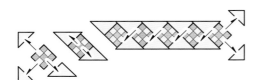

Make 2 side borders,
4¾" × 30¼".

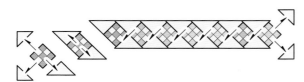

Make 2 top/bottom borders,
4¾" × 38¾".

⑤ Sew the muslin 2⅜" × 38¾" strips to opposite sides of the quilt top. Join the remaining muslin 2⅜"-wide strips end to end. From the pieced strip, cut two 42½"-long strips and sew them to the top and bottom of the quilt top. The quilt top should measure 42½" square, including seam allowances.

⑥ For border 6, join seven Star blocks to make a side border measuring 6½" × 42½", including seam allowances. Make two. Join nine Star blocks to make top/bottom borders measuring 6½" × 54½", including seam allowances. Sew border 6 to the sides first and then to the top and bottom of the quilt top. The quilt top should measure 54½" square, including seam allowances.

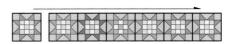

Make 2 side borders,
6½" × 42½".

Make 2 top/bottom borders,
6½" × 54½".

⑦ Join the muslin 3¼"-wide strips end to end. From the pieced strip, cut two 60"-long strips and two 54½"-long strips. Sew the shorter strips to opposite sides of the quilt top. Sew the longer strips to the top and bottom of the quilt top. The quilt top should measure 60" square, including seam allowances.

Making Border 8

① Join six A blocks, four gray or taupe squares, and five muslin side triangles in diagonal rows. Join the rows to make a center section. Make four sections.

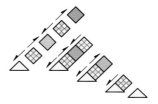

Center section.
Make 4 sections.

② Lay out eight A blocks, three gray or taupe squares, and the following muslin pieces: three 3½" squares, two 3½" × 9½" rectangles, one 3½" × 6½" rectangle, 13 side triangles, and one corner triangle. Sew the pieces into diagonal rows. Join the rows to make a side section. Make two. Make two reversed side sections, reversing the orientation of the pieces.

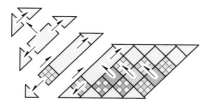

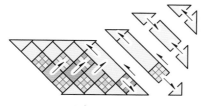

Side section.
Make 2 of each section.

3 Lay out 11 A blocks, four gray or taupe squares, and the following muslin pieces: five 3½" squares, four 3½" × 9½" rectangles, 18 side triangles, and one corner triangle. Sew the pieces into diagonal rows. Join the rows to make a top/bottom section. Make two. Make two reversed top/bottom sections, reversing the orientation of the pieces.

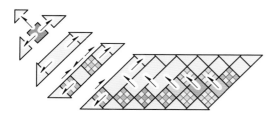

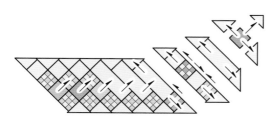

Top/bottom section.
Make 2 of each section.

4 Join a side section, a reversed side section, and a center section from step 1 to make a side border measuring 11⅛" × 60", including seam allowances. Make two. Join a top/bottom section, a reversed top/bottom section, and a center section to make the top border measuring 11⅛" × 81¼", including seam allowances. Repeat to make the bottom border.

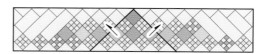

Make 2 side borders,
11⅛" × 60".

Make 2 top/bottom borders,
11⅛" × 81¼".

5 Sew border 8 to the sides first and then to the top and bottom of the quilt top. The quilt top should measure 81¼" square, including seam allowances. (See the tip box on page 54 to adjust the length of the borders if needed.)

Making the Outer Border

1 Sew a yellow star 1½"-wide strip to each long side of gray print 1½"-wide strip to make a strip set measuring 3½" × 42", including seam allowances. Make seven strip sets. Crosscut the strip sets into 164 segments, 1½" × 3½".

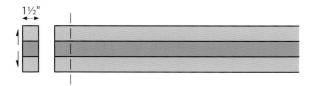

1½"

Make 7 strip sets, 3½" × 42".
Cut into 164 segments, 1½" × 3½".

2 Sew a muslin 1½"-wide strip to each long side of a yellow star 1½"-wide strip to make a strip set measuring 3½" × 42", including seam allowances. Make seven strip sets. Crosscut the strip sets into 164 segments, 1½" × 3½".

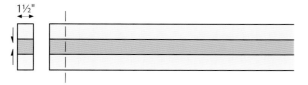

1½"

Make 7 strip sets, 3½" × 42".
Cut into 164 segments, 1½" × 3½".

3 Join two segments from step 1 and one segment from step 2 to make a border block measuring 3½" square, including seam allowances. Make 80 blocks.

Border block.
Make 80 blocks,
3½" × 3½".

4 Lay out three yellow star 1½" squares, two muslin 1½" squares, one gray print square, and one segment from step 1 in three rows. Sew the squares together into rows. Join the rows and step 1 segment to make a corner block measuring 3½" square, including seam allowances. Make four blocks.

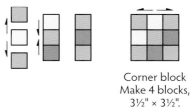

Corner block
Make 4 blocks,
3½" × 3½".

5 Join 21 segments from step 2 and 20 border blocks, alternating them as shown, to make a side border measuring 3½" × 81½". Make two. Make two top/bottom borders in the same way, adding a corner block to each end. The top and bottom borders should measure 3½" × 87½", including seam allowances.

Make 2 side borders,
3½" × 81½".

Make 2 top/bottom borders,
3½" × 87½".

Aa

is for Adjust to Fit

Mathematically some of the borders are ¼" longer than the quilt center. To get the borders to exactly fit, you may need to adjust their length. The easiest and least noticeable way to fine-tune the fit is by making some of the seam allowances in the border strips a tiny bit larger. Or, you may instead need to ease the quilt top to fit the borders.

6 Sew the side borders to the quilt top first, then add the top and bottom borders. The completed quilt top should measure 87¼" square.

Finishing the Quilt

For more details on any finishing steps, visit ShopMartingale.com/HowtoQuilt for free downloadable information.

1 Layer the backing, batting, and quilt top; baste.

2 Quilt by hand or machine. The quilt shown is machine quilted with an allover meandering design.

3 Use the taupe striped 2¼"-wide strips to make the binding, and then attach the binding to the quilt.

Quilt assembly

In the Ballpark

Watching a baseball game on a cool evening? Take this quilt with you to ward off the chill! Notice the balls and bats printed in the light fabric, and the four big squares in each block are like the bases.

Materials

Yardage is based on 42"-wide fabric.

- 2 yards *total* of assorted medium and dark prints for blocks and sashing (referred to collectively as "dark")
- 1¼ yards *total* of assorted cream prints for blocks and sashing
- 1⅜ yards of cream floral for sashing

- 2 yards of navy print for sashing, border, and binding
- 3½ yards of fabric for backing
- 63" × 73" piece of batting

Cutting

All measurements include ¼" seam allowances.

From the assorted dark prints, cut a *total* of:

10 strips, 1" × 42"; crosscut into 20 strips, 1" × 21"

120 squares, 3" × 3"

210 squares, 1½" × 1½"

150 squares, 1" × 1"

From the assorted cream prints, cut a *total* of:

20 strips, 1" × 42"; crosscut into 40 strips, 1" × 21"

168 squares, 1½" × 1½"

120 squares, 1" × 1"

From the cream floral, cut:

30 strips, 1½" × 42"

From the navy print, cut:

15 strips, 1½" × 42"

7 strips, 3½" × 42"

7 strips, 2¼" × 42"

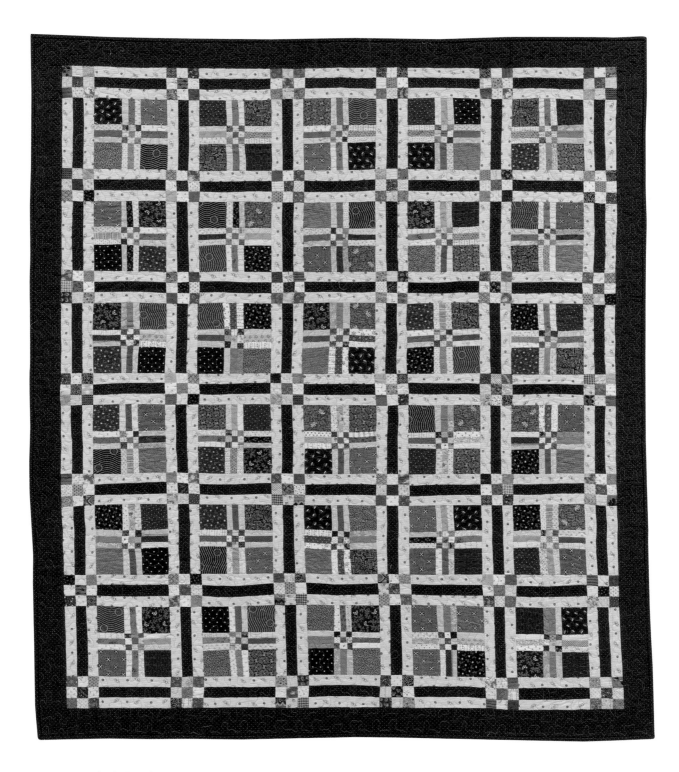

Finished quilt: 57" × 66½"   **Finished blocks: 6½" × 6½" and 3" × 3"**

Making the Golden Gate Blocks

Press all seam allowances in the directions indicated by the arrows.

1 Sew a cream print strip to each long side of a dark strip to make a strip set measuring 2" × 21", including seam allowances. Make a total of 20 strip sets. Crosscut the strip sets into 120 segments, 2" × 3".

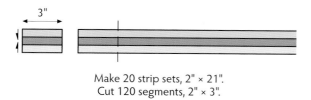

Make 20 strip sets, 2" × 21".
Cut 120 segments, 2" × 3".

2 Lay out five dark 1" squares and four cream print 1" squares in three rows. Sew the squares together into rows. Join the rows to make a nine-patch unit measuring 2" square, including seam allowances. Make 30 units.

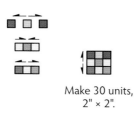

Make 30 units,
2" × 2".

3 Lay out four dark 3" squares, four segments from step 1, and one nine-patch unit from step 2 in three rows. Sew the pieces into rows. Join the rows to make a Golden Gate block measuring 7" square, including seam allowances. Make 30 blocks.

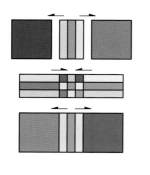

Make 30 blocks,
7" × 7".

Making the Sashing

1 Sew a cream floral strip to each long side of a navy 1½" × 42" strip to make a strip set measuring 3½" × 42", including seam allowances. Make a total of 15 strip sets. Crosscut the strip sets into 71 sashing segments, 3½" × 7".

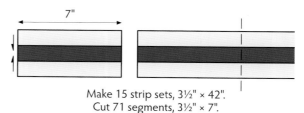

Make 15 strip sets, 3½" × 42".
Cut 71 segments, 3½" × 7".

2 Lay out five dark 1½" squares and four cream print 1½" squares in three rows. Sew the squares into rows. Join the rows to make a Nine Patch block measuring 3½" square, including seam allowances. Make 42 blocks.

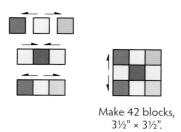

Make 42 blocks,
3½" × 3½".

Assembling the Quilt Top

1 Join six Nine Patch blocks and five sashing segments to make a sashing row measuring 3½" × 51", including seam allowances. Make seven rows.

Make 7 rows, 3½" × 51".

2 Join six sashing segments and five Golden Gate blocks to make a block row measuring 7" × 51", including seam allowances. Make six rows.

Make 6 rows, 7" × 51".

3 Join the sashing rows and block rows, alternating them as shown in the quilt assembly diagram below. The quilt-top center should measure 51" × 60½", including seam allowances.

4 Join the navy 3½"-wide strips end to end. From the pieced strip, cut two 60½"-long strips and two 57"-long strips. Sew the longer strips to opposite sides of the quilt top. Sew the shorter strips to the top and bottom. The completed quilt top should measure 57" × 66½".

Finishing the Quilt

For more details on any finishing steps, visit ShopMartingale.com/HowtoQuilt for free downloadable information.

1 Layer the backing, batting, and quilt top; baste.

2 Quilt by hand or machine. The quilt shown is machine quilted with an allover meandering design.

3 Use the navy 2¼"-wide strips to make the binding, and then attach the binding to the quilt.

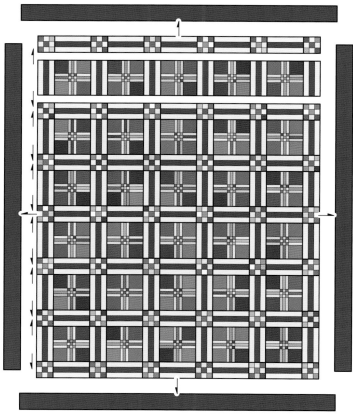

Quilt assembly

Lots of Dots

What's more cheerful than a super scrappy quilt with big dots! Notice how the dots are used sparingly in the alternate blocks; rather than appliquéing a dot to each square, I used them to fool your eye into seeing a medallion-type setting, with one dot in the center and the rest forming a large diamond pattern across the quilt top.

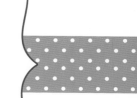

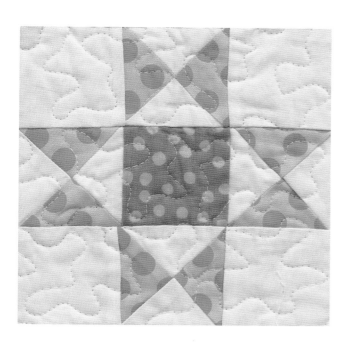

- 87" × 99" piece of batting
- Cardstock
- Spray starch

I cut the inner and middle borders from the lengthwise grain of the fabric. That way I could fussy cut the dots and use one row of large dots in the inner border and four rows of smaller dots in the middle border. If you prefer to cut the strips from the crosswise grain, see "B is for Border Option" below for the amount of yardage and number of strips you'll need.

Materials

Yardage is based on 42"-wide fabric.

- 4 yards *total* of assorted medium and dark prints for blocks and setting squares (referred to collectively as "dark")
- 1⅜ yards *total* of assorted light prints for blocks and setting squares
- 3½ yards of white solid for blocks
- 2⅜ yards of red-and-white dot for inner border*
- 2½ yards of cream dot for middle border*
- ⅝ yard of red print for binding
- 7¼ yards of fabric for backing

Bb
is for Border Option

The materials list allows enough fabric to cut border strips lengthwise. If you prefer to cut crosswise-grain border strips, you can use less fabric. Here's what you'll need:

Inner border: ½ yard of red-and-white dot; cut 8 strips, 1½" × 42"

Middle border: 1 yard of cream dot; cut 9 strips, 3½" × 42"

For each border, join the strips end to end. From the pieced strips, cut strips to the lengths specified in "Cutting" on page 63.

Cutting

All measurements include ¼" seam allowances.

From the assorted dark prints, cut a *total* of:

38 squares, 6½" × 6½"

113 sets of 2 matching squares, 3¼" × 3¼" (226 total); cut the squares into quarters diagonally to yield 904 triangles (keep like triangles together)

72 squares, 2½" × 2½"

From the assorted light prints, cut a *total* of:

33 squares, 6½" × 6½"

From the white solid, cut:

19 strips, 3¼" × 42"; crosscut into 226 squares, 3¼" × 3¼". Cut the squares into quarters diagonally to yield 904 triangles.

20 strips, 2½" × 42"; crosscut into 288 squares, 2½" × 2½".

From the *lengthwise* grain of the red-and-white dot, cut:

2 strips, 1½" × 78½"

2 strips, 1½" × 68½"

From the *lengthwise* grain of the cream dot, cut:

2 strips, 3½" × 80½"

2 strips, 3½" × 74½"

From the red print, cut:

9 strips, 2¼" × 42"

Making the Ohio Star Blocks

Press all seam allowances in the directions indicated by the arrows.

1 Lay out two white triangles and two matching dark triangles in alternating positions. Sew the triangles into pairs. Join the pairs to make an hourglass unit measuring 2½" square, including seam allowances. Make 452 units.

Make 452 units, 2½" × 2½".

2 Lay out four white 2½" squares, four matching hourglass units, and one dark 2½" square in three rows. Sew the pieces into rows. Join the rows to make a block measuring 6½" square, including seam allowances. Make 72 blocks. You'll have 164 hourglass units left over to use for the outer border.

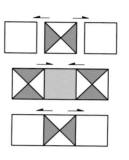 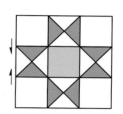

Make 72 blocks, 6½" × 6½".

Making the Appliquéd Blocks

1 Use the patterns on page 67 to trace 22 large circles and one small circle onto cardstock. Cut out the circles on the traced lines. Trace the large and small circles onto the wrong side of seven different dark prints, leaving at least ⅝" between them. Cut out the circles, adding a generous ¼" seam allowance to each.

2 Sew a long running stitch around the edges of a circle on the right side of the fabric, about ³⁄₁₆" in from the edge. Don't knot the start or end; instead, leave a long tail at each end. Place the cardstock template in the center of the marked circle. Gently pull the thread tails to gather the fabric over the template until it's evenly gathered and taut around the edge of the circle. Smooth out any puckers on the edge. Tie off the threads to hold the gathering firmly in place. Spray with starch and press well. Repeat for the remaining circles.

3 Gently remove the cardstock template from the circles. Tighten the gathering stitches if required to reshape the circles.

4 Referring to the photo on page 65, position a large circle in the center of a dark 6½" square. (Fold the square in half vertically and horizontally to find the center.) Appliqué the circle in place. Make 22 blocks.

Make 22 blocks,
6½" × 6½".

5 Position the small circle in the center of a light 6½" square. Appliqué the circle in place.

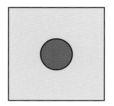

Make 1 block,
6½" × 6½".

Making the Outer Border

1 Join 43 hourglass units, rotating every other unit, to make a side border measuring 2½" × 86½", including seam allowances. Make two.

Make 2 side borders,
2½" × 86½".

2 Join 39 hourglass units, rotating every other unit, to make the top border measuring 2½" × 78½", including seam allowances. Repeat to make the bottom border.

Make 2 top/bottom borders,
2½" × 78½".

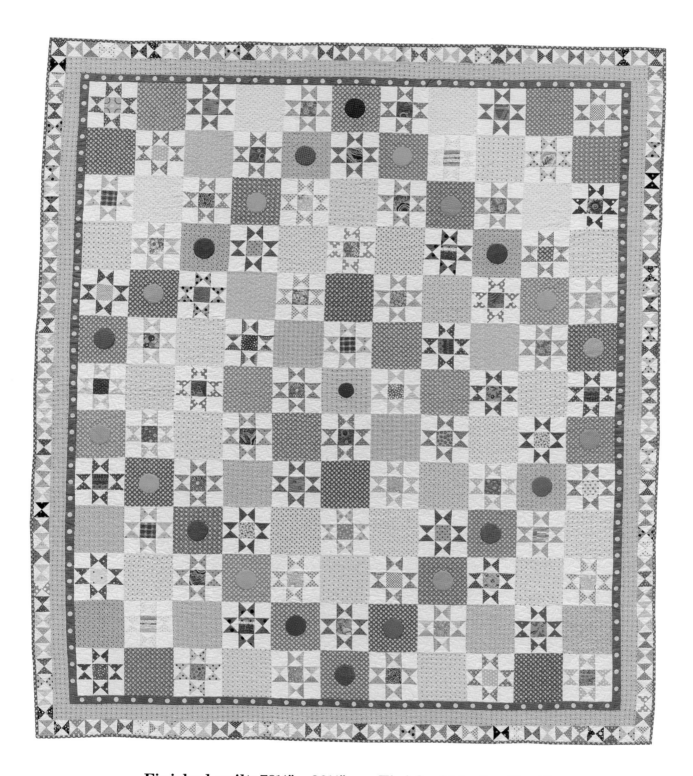

Finished quilt: 78½" × 90½"   **Finished blocks: 6" × 6"**

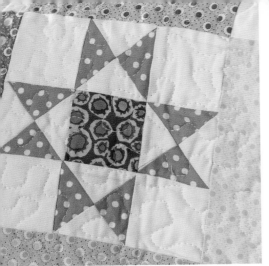

Assembling the Quilt Top

Refer to the quilt assembly diagram below and the quilt photo as needed.

1 Lay out the Ohio Star blocks, the light and dark 6½" squares, and the appliquéd blocks in 13 rows of 11 blocks each, making sure to place the appliquéd block with the small circle in the quilt center. Sew the blocks into rows. Join the rows to make the quilt-top center measuring 66½" × 78½", including seam allowances.

2 Sew the red-and-white 1½" × 78½" strips to opposite sides of the quilt top. Sew the red-and-white 1½" × 68½" strips to the top and bottom. The quilt top should measure 68½" × 80½", including seam allowances.

3 Sew the cream 3½" × 80½" strips to opposite sides of the quilt top. Sew the cream 3½" × 74½" strips to the top and bottom. The quilt top should measure 74½" × 86½", including seam allowances.

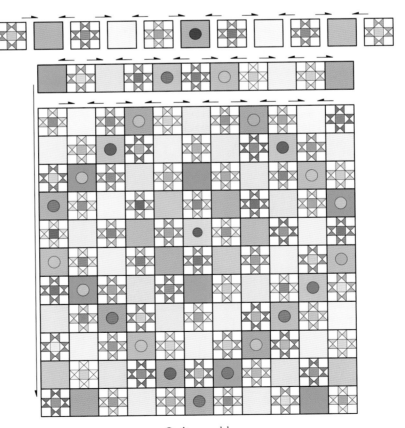

Quilt assembly

4 Sew the side outer borders to the quilt first, and then add the top and bottom outer borders. The completed quilt top should measure 78½" × 90½".

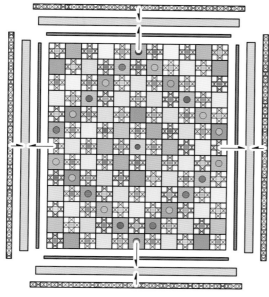

Adding the borders

Finishing the Quilt

For details on finishing steps, visit ShopMartingale.com/HowtoQuilt for free downloadable information.

1 Layer the backing, batting, and quilt top; baste.

2 Quilt by hand or machine. The quilt shown is machine quilted with an allover meandering design.

3 Use the red print 2¼"-wide strips to make the binding, and then attach the binding to the quilt.

Patterns do not include seam allowances.

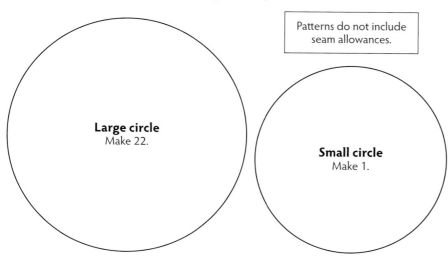

Large circle
Make 22.

Small circle
Make 1.

Jardin Lattice

I love everything about French provincial fabrics. The vivid primary colors, the use of paisley motifs large and small, and the wonderful mix of florals, from whimsical to realistic—what's not to love? To showcase these stunning fabrics, I cut them into large diamonds and used the colors to define a diamond-shaped medallion look.

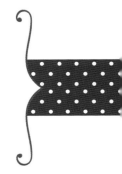

Materials

Yardage is based on 42"-wide fabric.

- 2¾ yards *total* of assorted red, gold, blue, green, purple, and black prints for diamonds and setting triangles
- 2¼ yards of cream floral for sashing
- 2⅝ yards of red stripe for border
- ⅝ yard of green print for binding
- 5⅜ yards of fabric for backing
- 71" × 95" piece of batting
- Template plastic

Cutting

Before you begin cutting, trace patterns A–D on pages 73 and 74 onto template plastic and cut them out. Use the templates to cut the A–D pieces from fabrics listed below. All measurements include ¼" seam allowances.

From the assorted prints, cut a *total* of:

72 of piece A (12 red, 4 gold, 20 blue, and 36 from remaining prints)

12 of piece B

10 of piece C

2 of piece D

2 of piece D reversed

From the cream floral, cut:

35 strips, 2" × 42"; crosscut into the following lengths, noting that for strips marked with an asterisk (*), you'll need to piece strips together to achieve the required measurement:

  1 strip, 2" × 92"*

  2 strips, 2" × 85"*

  2 strips, 2" × 72"*

  2 strips, 2" × 57"*

  2 strips, 2" × 40"

  2 strips, 2" × 27"

  2 strips, 2" × 13"

  84 strips, 2" × 7½"

From the *lengthwise* grain of the red stripe, cut:

2 strips, 7" × 89"

2 strips, 7" × 68"

From the green print, cut:

8 strips, 2¼" × 42"

Assembling the Quilt Top

Press all seam allowances in the directions indicated by the arrows.

1 Lay out the A–D pieces and cream strips in diagonal rows as shown in the quilt assembly diagram below. Sew the pieces into rows, referring to step 2, right, for aligning and trimming the sashing. To form the medallion look, carefully place the assorted print diamonds so you have four gold in the center, surrounded by 12 red diamonds. Surround that with 20 blue diamonds. The remaining diamonds are placed randomly.

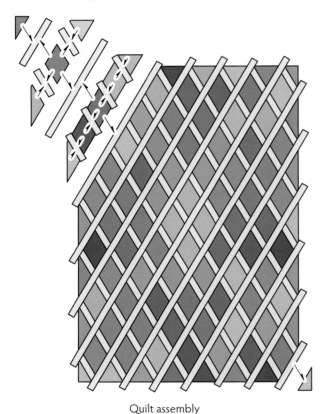

Quilt assembly

2 When sewing the short cream strips to the diamonds, place them so the ends of the cream strips extend ⅜" beyond the edge of the diamonds. Sew, press, and then trim the ends of the cream strips even with the edges of the diamond pieces. Press and trim as you go to making aligning the diamonds easier.

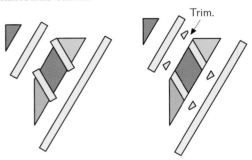

Trim.

Mm
is for Match It Up

When joining block rows and long sashing strips, it's important that the short vertical sashing strips correctly line up on each side of the long sashing strip. An easy way to make the strips line up is to mark the long strips with pins to show the junctions that must match. Sew one edge of the long strip to a block row. Then pin-mark the other edge of the long strip. Join the long strip and block row, matching the seam junctions with the pins.

Finished quilt: 62½" × 86"

5 Center and then sew the red 89"-long strips to opposite sides of the quilt, stopping ¼" from each corner. Center and sew the red 68"-long strips to the top and bottom of the quilt, again stopping ¼" from each corner. Use your preferred method to miter the corners. For more help with the mitered borders, go to ShopMartingale.com/HowtoQuilt. The completed quilt top should measure 62½" × 86".

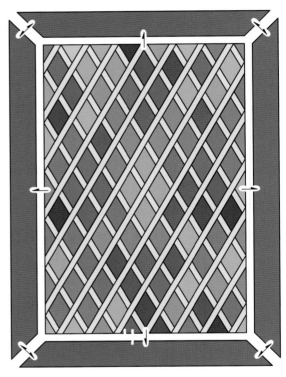

Adding the borders

3 Join the rows and long cream strips to make the quilt-top center. Pin match the seam intersections across the sashing rows so that the diamonds line up completely.

4 Trim the ends of the sashing strips even with the edges of the diamond pieces around the perimeter. The quilt top should measure 49½" × 73", including seam allowances.

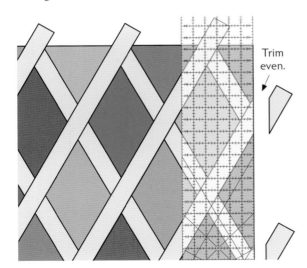

Trim even.

Finishing the Quilt

For more details on any finishing steps, visit ShopMartingale.com/HowtoQuilt for free downloadable information.

1 Layer the backing, batting, and quilt top; baste.

2 Quilt by hand or machine. The quilt shown is machine quilted with an allover meandering design.

3 Use the green 2¼"-wide strips to make the binding, and then attach the binding to the quilt.

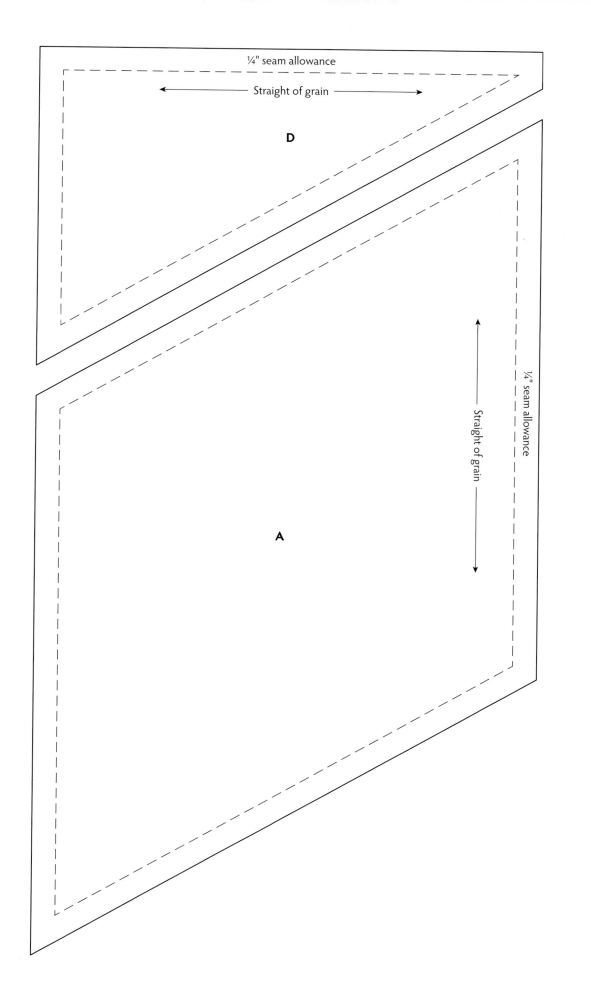

¼" seam allowance

Straight of grain

D

¼" seam allowance

Straight of grain

A

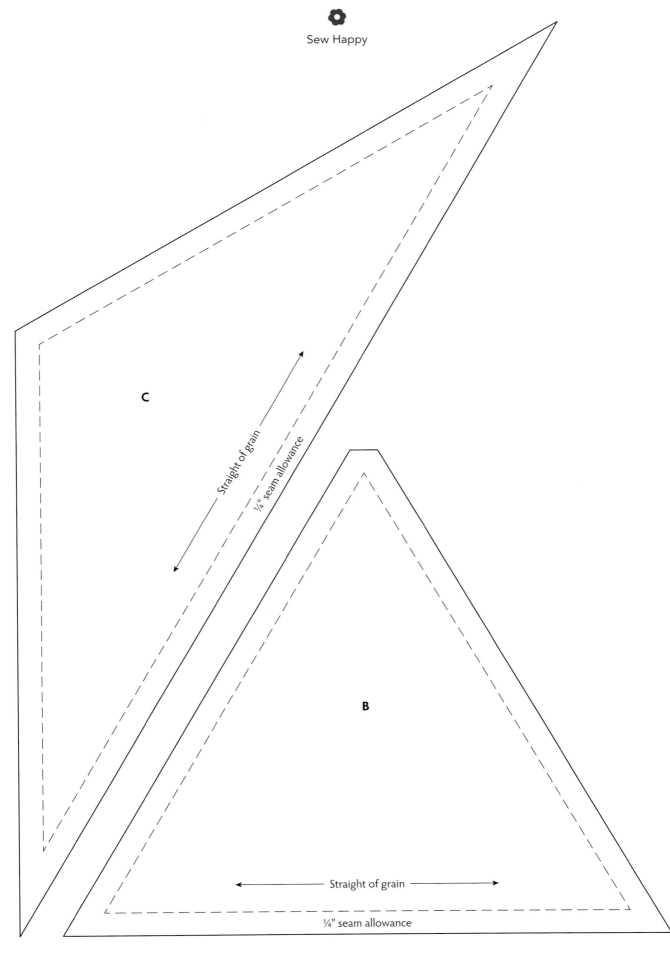

C

Straight of grain

¼" seam allowance

B

Straight of grain

¼" seam allowance

Mrs. Sippi

Mrs. Sippi: The name was inspired by a quilt I saw in a book from the state of Mississippi. I loved learning how to spell Mississippi in elementary school, so I named this quilt Mrs. Sippi!

Materials

Yardage is based on 42"-wide fabric.

- 2⅜ yards *total* of assorted cream prints for blocks
- 2⅜ yards *total* of assorted red prints for blocks
- 3 yards of yellow print for sashing
- 1 yard of green print for sashing squares
- ⅞ yard of pink print for border*

- ⅝ yard of red print for binding
- 7½ yards of fabric for backing
- 90" × 90" piece of batting

If you wish to cut strips from the lengthwise grain, you'll need 2½ yards. Refer to step 4 of "Assembling the Quilt Top" to cut the strips to the correct length.

Cutting

All measurements include ¼" seam allowances.

From the assorted cream prints, cut a *total* of:
144 sets of 2 matching squares, 3" × 3" (288 total)

From the assorted red prints, cut a *total* of:
144 sets of 2 matching squares, 3" × 3" (288 total)

From the yellow print, cut:
21 strips, 4½" × 42"; crosscut into 84 rectangles, 4½" × 8½"

From the green print, cut:
7 strips, 4½" × 42"; crosscut into 49 squares, 4½" × 4½"

From the pink print, cut:
9 strips, 3" × 42"

From the red print for binding, cut:
9 strips, 2¼" × 42"

Making the Blocks

Press all seam allowances in the directions indicated by the arrows.

1 Draw a diagonal line from corner to corner on the wrong side of the cream 3" squares. Layer a marked square on a red 3" square, right sides together. Sew ¼" from both sides of the drawn line. Cut the unit apart on the marked line to make two half-square-triangle units. Trim the units to measure 2½" square, including seam allowances. Make 576 units, keeping like units together.

Make 576 units.

2 Lay out four matching half-square-triangle units in two rows of two, orienting the units to form a pinwheel as shown. Sew the units into rows. Join the rows to make a pinwheel unit measuring 4½" square, including seam allowances. Make 144 units.

Make 144 units, 4½" × 4½".

Pp

is for Pressing Pinwheels

When it comes to pressing Pinwheel blocks, I press all of the seam allowances to one side. I'm traditional like that! But some quilters prefer a flatter block center, so you could also press the seam allowances open—the choice is yours.

3 Lay out four pinwheel units in two rows of two. You can use matching units or four different units. (The featured quilt uses both strategies; see the photo on page 78.) Sew the units together into rows. Join the rows to make a block measuring 8½" square, including seam allowances. Make 36 blocks.

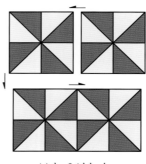

Make 36 blocks, 8½" × 8½".

Assembling the Quilt Top

1 Join seven green squares and six yellow rectangles to make a sashing row measuring 4½" × 76½", including seam allowances. Make seven rows.

Make 7 rows, 4½" × 76½".

2 Join seven yellow rectangles and six blocks to make a block row measuring 8½" × 76½", including seam allowances. Make six rows.

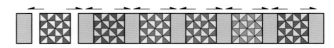

Make 6 rows, 8½" × 76½".

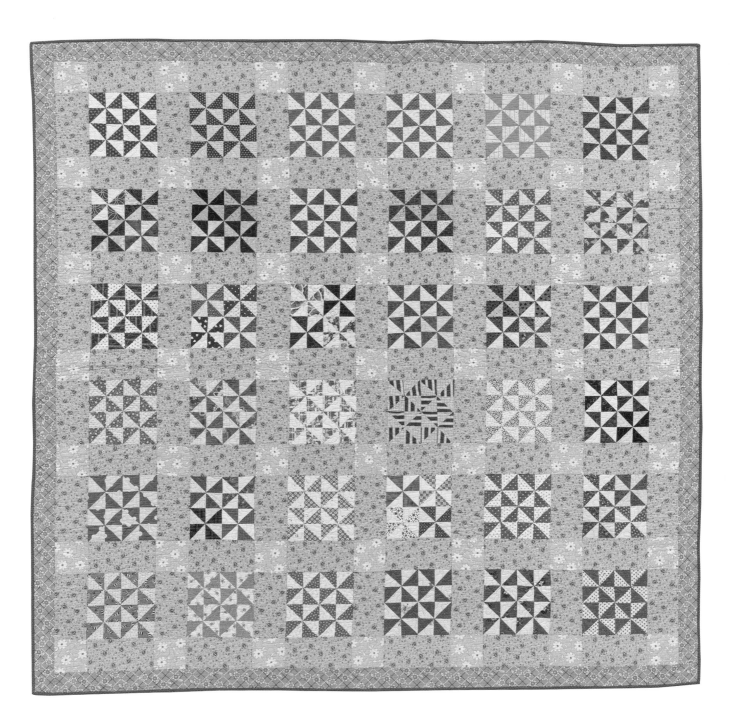

Finished quilt: 81½" × 81½"   **Finished blocks: 8" × 8"**

3 Join the sashing rows and block rows, alternating them as shown in the quilt assembly diagram below. The quilt-top center should measure 76½" square, including seam allowances.

4 Join the pink 3"-wide strips end to end. From the pieced strip, cut two 81½"-long strips and two 76½"-long strips. Sew the shorter strips to the top and bottom of the quilt top. Sew the longer strips to the sides. The completed quilt top should measure 81½" square.

Finishing the Quilt

For more details on any finishing steps, visit ShopMartingale.com/HowtoQuilt for free downloadable information.

1 Layer the backing, batting, and quilt top; baste.

2 Quilt by hand or machine. The quilt shown is machine quilted with an allover meandering design.

3 Use the red 2¼"-wide strips to make the binding, and then attach the binding to the quilt.

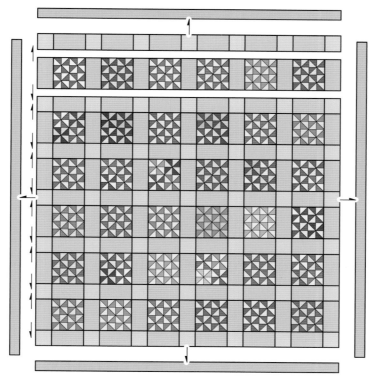

Quilt assembly

Acknowledgments

It takes several people to produce a book. I get my name on the cover, but there are other people who make it happen. I was a little hesitant when Karen Soltys first approached me about writing a book. With her encouragement and offer to help, I agreed—and the team at Martingale went to work on my behalf. A sincere thank-you goes to Karen Soltys, Tina Cook, Laurie Baker, Nancy Mahoney, Melissa Bryan, Adrienne Smitke, Regina Girard, Mia Mar, Brent Kane, Sandy Loi, Bree Larson, and Stephanie Sullivan. I'm very grateful for all of your hard work!

~ Sandy

About the Author

The creative mind behind American Jane Patterns, Sandy Klop is known for colorfully scrappy quilts with an upbeat traditional look. As a longtime designer for Moda Fabrics, Sandy renders cheerily nostalgic prints in rich primary colors.

Sandy was trained as an art teacher and began quilting while living in Iran and then Saudi Arabia, teaching at an American school. After moving back to the United States, she continued to build her interest in quilting, eventually launching American Jane Patterns, selling quilt kits, teaching quiltmaking, and sharing her patterns in a variety of quilting magazines. Visit Sandy at AmericanJane.com.